MY STEINWAY BLUES

*Copyright © 2011 Anthony Sharp.
All rights reserved*

No part of this book may be reproduced, stored in a retrievable system, or transmitted by any means without the written permission of the author.

ISBN: 978-1461060291

ALSO BY ANTHONY SHARP

The Guv′nor

The House Of Baghdad

Lie Back & Think Of England

Now Or Never

To Mama With Love

My Steinway Blues

A True Story

Anthony Sharp

AUTHOR'S NOTE

For years it was generally considered by our venerable elders that no one should publish an autobiography until he or she is ready to drop dead. How times have changed. Yet in my own case, the original 'decency' probably applies. In fact, not so long ago a rumour went round the Spanish coastal town where I had resided for many moons that I had indeed fallen off my proverbial perch. When I suddenly appeared in the doorway of the English newsagent in the street where I had owned a piano bar, the girl behind the counter turned ashen white and nearly dropped the paper she was about to sell to an innocent customer.

'I've just come off the cross,' I brightly announced in Jewish mimicry. 'A little bit of *blood*.., but nothing too serious.'

She smiled awkwardly at my tasteless remarks, though I suspect she was glad I actually bought a paper and gave her the correct money – if only to convince her I was real and not an overly playful apparition. Just as well I had already written part of my story, I thought, since one day my passing will no longer be mere rumour.

Anthony Sharp

ACKNOWLEGEMENTS

My thanks, as always, to my friend George V. Scott who remains tireless in his support and encouragement to an old sod like me.

To my own nephew Dr John Butt, a brilliant musician and scholar, at the time of writing The Gardiner Professor of Music at Glasgow University, for his encouragement and for proofreading my manuscript.

And to my agent in the sky.

Some personal and place names have been changed in this book – for the usual reasons

To my darling Tabsy -

my soul mate

CHAPTER 1

How often, long ago, would those eager young lungs burst forth with song, and a treble voice soar with such delight... My soul doth magnify The Lord. And my spirit hath rejoiced in God, my saviour.

If only I could believe. But I want to believe, if only to make sense of the mess.

Turning East, I would trot out The Creed: I believe in One God, The Father Almighty...The Holy Catholic Church worried me. The Rector of the parish insisted it meant The 'Universal Church', though with his surveilling eye and a strange whiff of incense about his person, I could never be quite sure. For even as an eleven year-old choirboy in the local church, I harboured serious doubts about what I was doing... Do I really believe this stuff? Or has The Establishment, a decent 'middle-class' upbringing and a need to cling to something beyond the norm seduced me into submissiveness? Is it just the music, the sound of the organ, the buzz, the elitism that draws me?

I believe in God The Father, God The Son, and God The Holy Ghost... Now, *there's* a fascinating concept for an imaginative youngster. Not any old ghost, but a *holy* one... Maybe life itself is a dream, and the hereafter the real thing. I do hope so; even hoped so as an eleven year-old. For I clearly recall looking up at the stars one night, and saying to myself: 'What the hell am I doing here again?' Not that I was prepared to top myself at that age. There must have been a reason why I was here again. There is always hope.

Faith, hope and charity. I assumed if you had hope, you didn't need the faith. Or was it the other way round? But charity or love. Wow. That's a difficult one these days – in a consumer-mad society. Back in the early 50s, after a bloody war with Germany, people still seemed prepared to be kind and show care for one another, almost as if the war had not ended... The hedonist 60s and 70s were a long way off, the twenty-first century inconceivable. It was sweet rations, three-penny bits, the first taste of Italian ice-cream in Leytonstone High Road for us grateful lot.

In nearby Wanstead, where we lived on and off during the war, life had 'progressed' from good old Cockney accents, pie and mash, jellied eels and the like. Those who lived in Hoxton, Bow, Poplar or even Leytonstone viewed Wanstead people as toffs, never having met a real one. We were, at best, snobs. But like the true Cockneys, we too had to duck for the bombs and dive for the 'doodle-bugs'. I never forget my family and me rushing out into the street to witness our first flying bomb, the V1. 'Hey, look at that funny-looking plane.' Then the engine cut out, the 'plane' dropped from the sky, and some poor sod took the brunt of the bomb. Mr Hitler's "spiffing" new invention had altered the ethos of the war. The V2s would come next, silent and lethal, without warning.

But we all remember the V1s or 'doodle-bugs'. I recall one day my sister Pat, standing at the top of the stairs that led to our cellar where we kept the coal. Father had made a level floor of strong boards on top of which we piled thick blankets, pillows and such for comfortable shelter and 'sleep' during raids on London. But now, as we waited – my parents and other sister Hazel – for the approaching doodle-bug to do its worst on Wanstead or elsewhere, we wondered why Pat remained hesitant to join us below. Just then, the engine stopped, the bomb exploded, and the blast did the rest. 'Hallo,' said Pat casually with a grin, as she was miraculously blown down the stairs, landing unhurt on a spare blanket.

My dad must have been psychic or just bloody lucky. How we all thanked him for making those boards, for the very first night we slept down the cellar, an ordinary bomb – dropped 'by hand', as it were – demolished two houses behind ours, killing everyone inside. We would have been cut to pieces but for my father's intuition and initiative.

On another occasion, I was out with my mother, doing a bit of shopping in East Ham High Street when the siren started its awful wailing, a terrifying sound for us young kids. We dodged into the nearest shelter which quickly filled up with anxious people, caught on the hop. As more and more entered the reinforced shelter, my mother took me by the hand and made for the exit.

'You're very silly, madam,' exhorted the air-raid warden. 'They'll be over here in a minute.'

'Bugger that,' shouted back my mother. 'Come along, Tony. We'll jump on a bus, and get home.'

Bless her. The hunch saved our lives. It was not so funny for those poor people in the shelter. The next morning we read in the paper a bomb had dropped on the place, and killed all those who had chosen to stay.

And then, in 1945, came Victory in Europe. Victory in Japan, as far as we were concerned, could wait. As Londoners, it was the Jerries who interested us. They were beaten again, and we wanted to let go a bit, and celebrate.

Out came the big Union Jack, strung across the road for all to see. Out came the tables and chairs in a long row down the street… Then spam, spam, spam, even a little black market ham; corned beef, of course, eggs and cheese. My father even killed a few of his precious chickens to add to the feast. Jellies for us kids, mince pies… What war? And then the music: MacNamarra's Band, the crocodile dance. Dancing from house to house. Laughter, laughter, beer, whisky...

And then it was all over. The tables and chairs were packed and taken away, the scraps, the plates and cutlery, the jugs and bottles. A few vows to keep in touch or meet at the pub, a few tears of joy and a few tears of woe for lost ones in the fighting. And then it was over. We all disappeared into our own homes, and waited for the next big war. We are still waiting, thank Heavens.

Yes, I've said it before: the Brits are not very good at peace. We are best at war. Or acting. Not much else.

'Oh, that's a bit hard,' I hear you mutter. But just consider the idea for a moment... The Latins are so good at living; not very good at war. The French let everyone down, and look after themselves. The Spanish Empire is long gone, their Civil War still hurts and lingers in the memory of some families, even now. What do *they* want with war? The Italians run away.

An Italian friend said to me a while ago, when I painted this sweeping picture... 'Oh, you British. You are made for war. *We* are made for *love.*'

How could I argue with that? Bless you, Lucio, the man who when discussing my capacity for alcohol, made the encouraging remark: 'When God made you, Tony, He forgot to put the liver in.' A novel idea. Yet, somehow even Lucio may be proved wrong one day. My medics in Spain have already warned me, and I *have* cut back on my intake: for the time being.

But to return to the early years after the war.., the church services, my Grammar School, clandestine sexual fumblings ('Stop that, Sharp'), looking out for the new cars, all painted black, of course, Eddy Bradley's brand new Hillman Minx, 1946 model...

When Eddy, a good drinking pal of my father, proudly drew up outside his house opposite ours, he opened the car door which promptly fell off in his hand, crashing dramatically into the roadway. Maybe the war hadn't quite ended, after all. We didn't have to wait for the British Leyland era for 'jerry-built' to become a popular phrase. But we laughed about it, and Eddy's door was fixed.

When I'd reached the age of twelve, it was decided that my first piano teacher, Mrs Wyebrow – doubtless a decent, upstanding woman – would never be in the league of inspiring teachers of the art. She had, it seemed, a more important programme lined up for her young charge. A buxom lady, to say the least, she pointedly positioned a handsome photo of Winston Churchill on the top of her upright piano. Since my seventh birthday, she had bombarded me with facts, figures and admiration for the great man – in preparation, it would appear in hindsight, for the unforgivable, *huge* red poster, shamelessly displayed in our front window after the war: **VOTE LABOUR**.

How could The Sharps do such a terrible thing? I could see them through the net curtains: the neighbours, pointing indignantly at the hideous disfiguration and insult to Mr Churchill. 'Look at *that*. That's The Sharps for you. Disgusting. After *all* Winnie did for us.'

But my father had fought in Gallipoli. He had fought in that terrible battle of The First World War, killed Turkish men in hand to hand combat: bayoneted the poor sods to death. It was a case of survival.

'How could you do it, dad?' I innocently asked over the dinner table.

'Tony, it was him or me. If I hadn't killed him first, I would not be your father, and you wouldn't be sitting here with me, eating this mutton and onion sauce.'

I had to admit, the mutton and onion sauce *did* taste delicious. My father had made his point, and I went on to other matters...

'So, how did you find this new piano teacher, dad?'

Mr Wagstaff of Buckhurst Hill, Essex, radiated music, charm and life. He was a very good teacher, and kept himself in physical shape for the job.

'You have to be fit for music, my boy,' he said as he whisked up to me one Saturday morning on his bike, dead on time for my lesson. He knew his housekeeper would let me in, but he preferred to keep his side of the bargain. He was right about physical fitness, too. Not that he would ever be required to lug heavy Fender Rhodes electric pianos to funky gigs all over London. How could he foretell my bohemian lifestyle, after I had exhausted or rather fouled up my classical career? Yet he felt it his job to prepare me for the physical, mental and emotional strains put upon any musician worth his salt. My father's background of hard work, "battling on", bayoneting and a certain amount of drinking would also contribute to my future strengths.

So music was not a sissy's profession, after all, despite remorseless quips from school masters. As for tennis. 'Tennis? You want to play tennis? It's a girl's game, Sharp. This is a rugger and cricket school.'

I was denied the chance to play tennis on the school courts, strictly reserved for the girls. Unimaginative fools... 'Music? Music is for...' Ah, sod 'em, I thought. Crude, uncultured lot. It's a wonder England ever produced a single composer. In the sixteenth century, of course, it was expected of a gentleman to be able to sight-read madrigals round the table after dinner. In my humble opinion, Queen Elizabeth The First was England's greatest monarch, for many a reason.

Look at the culture then: Shakespeare, Marlowe, Bacon and a host of others. Fine musicians abounded, and world-class composers. How many people who live in England today, I wonder, have heard of Orlando Gibbons, William Byrd, John Morley, Thomas Tomkins? The list goes on... Beautiful, highly imaginative music, much of which surpassed the continental style in richness of harmony and counterpoint. And as for the madrigals, some of the naughty lyrics, subtly implied through the counterpoint, might stir even today's censors into action – if only they could spot the subtlety.

Queen Elizabeth was not her father's daughter for nothing. Not only did she preside over a flourishing era of literature and music, but she saw off those darned foreigners. Spain and Popery could go to hell, as far as she was concerned. And to show she meant business, off would come her cousin Mary's head. The great storm off the east coast of England in July 1588 would do the rest. Philip The Second of Spain was not only rather cross with God at the time, but with a shifty Pope who refused to honour his pledge to pick up the tab for the huge fleet, now scattered and reduced to wrecks in the cold northern seas of Europe. To poor Philip's mind, if not the Pope's, there should never have been a question as to whose side God would choose to attach himself. Lucky for England, God has a mind of his own. MAGNIFICAT.

CHAPTER 2

'Oh, he's a politically incorrect writer, is he?' Methinks thou protesteth too much...
POLITICALLY INCORRECT? What the hell does this mean? Does it mean the denial of free speech, an insidious reversal of prejudices, or worse for the future of education: the prohibition of the study of history?

I know someone (she can't be alone) who almost violently attacks a genuine interest in history, and relegates it to the bin. Only the daily paper, her 'bible', is to be trusted. With due respect to the business acumen and success of her particular 'bible', God help us all.

For me, it all began round the breakfast table of Number 39, Woodcote Road.

Mother and father were diametrically opposed in almost every way. Yet there was no rancour, violence or foul language, spat out in uncontrolled bitterness. Ideas of general philosophy, beliefs, education and so on were discussed freely, and I could pick out the bits I liked, and discard or shelve the others for another day.

'Education is the most important ingredient in life,' my father would postulate.

'No. Personality is much more important,' my mother would respond with conviction. I had already decided to plump for both. I'm not sure I've done a good job of the experiment, but it's been a nice try. If I had to choose one against the other, perhaps my mother had the right idea. But a nation neglects education at its peril.

Take England, for instance. Education has been pulled from pillar to post by both main political parties…

What ever happened to the Grammar schools? They did a wonderful job, elevating the poorer classes from the mire of mediocrity to standards of excellence – through universities and colleges and on into the wider world. Then the silly critics of supposed elitism called for an umbrella of uniformity under which every child could feel safe. Balderdash; but sadly translated into an indiscriminate destruction of fine, individual schools – in favour of social factories, content with compromised standards in place of high, internationally recognized attainments.

Sorry, folks. You can offer equal opportunities for all, but in the end we are simply not equal. "All animals are equal but some animals are more equal than others". George Orwell's famous lines give one the cruel facts of life.

I looked up again at the photograph on the wall by the front door of Number 39 – at the school photo of Christ's Hospital, Horsham, and the picture of my cousin as a small boy in the front row.

'That's where I'd like you to go, mate,' said my father, rather roughly, I thought, one Sunday morning before he set off for the pub to join his drinking pals.

It had been intimated to me through members of the family that my dad, as a survivor of Gallipoli, a Freeman of The City of London, and a one-time active member of four lodges would have little difficulty in procuring for me an entrance to the famous public school where a number of places were traditionally reserved for sons of the poor or other such deserving folk.

'I don't want to wear those silly yellow stockings, mum,' I pleaded more than once. 'Nor those cassocks.'

'Well, don't make him, Billy,' cooed my mother. 'Let him go to the local Grammar.'

My father never forgave my mum for siding with me. Nor could he really comprehend, understandably, the difference between wearing those school clothes and a cassock and surplice which I wore quite happily every Sunday as a choirboy in the local church. But children, like many parents, are strange creatures, and who knows what governs their complex thoughts and fears? I suppose I accepted the idea of dressing up for an hour or so in church: maybe The Holy Ghost would accept such attire, and even put in a quick appearance if I wore it. But the thought of wearing that strange school uniform all day long was too much. Then what would happen at night-time in the dormitory? Now, now.

So, to the local Grammar I went – Wanstead County High School for boys and girls, Redbridge Lane, Wanstead (now Comprehensive, of course). The Headmaster, a gruff Edwardian figure called Mr Joseph remained the boss for my first two years there, to be replaced by a charming, liberal yet strong Mr Ingham who took a personal interest in every pupil – more than 750 of us: big for a grammar school of its day. He knew every one of us by our Christian names, too, and would kindly explain why he had to cane us – if such a misfortune should come our way.

But bloody Sharp, young as he was, and ever the mimic, got away with it.

'I'm sorry I can't cane you, today,' he said, gently putting his arm round my shoulder like a trusted uncle. 'But I have a meeting with The Governors. Come back on Wednesday morning, and we'll sort it out then.'

Wonderful stuff. Sorting it out, by the way, was not, in Arthur Ingham's case, a euphemism for a good thrashing, but more an enquiry into the circumstances of a particular master's report.

On Wednesday morning I duly arrived with my partner-in-crime, a boy whose name I forget. The Headmaster asked me to explain what I had done. I was only too pleased to enact the situation. This was Sharp, the frustrated actor – at last given his head, and if he acted it well, he'd save the sanctity of his bottom a while longer...

I made the other boy get up on a spare, convenient chair which I persuaded Mr Ingham was essential for the act to be fully appreciated. With the boy looking rather red and awkward up there, young Sharp took a fiendish delight in mimicking to perfection yet another master's intonation and stance. 'Come down from there, boy!' I did all the body movements, too. Mr Ingham, I suspected, enjoyed the whole performance, but naturally felt duty bound to control the beginnings of a wide, responsive smile. Nevertheless, I'd made it.

'Is that all you were doing?'

'Yes, sir.'

'All right. One hundred lines of Latin verse by tomorrow after school.'

My partner-in-crime smirked as privately as possible and was let off.

How was I to know the same headmaster would give me a crash course of Latin in order to get me into Oxford a few years later? Maybe he had his eye on me in those early years, though it would be a battle of wills and political bias as to the wisdom of going to an old university, rather than a London college of music. By the time I'd reached the fifth form, I knew what I wanted.

CHAPTER 3

From the very beginning, my grammar school posed both a perceived threat to my well-being and an opportunity to develop whatever powers I had inherited from my parents and ancestors. Lessons and homework apart, I soon determined to keep my eye on the pursuit of happiness, or at least the avoidance of unnecessary, emotional stress or physical damage.

Since I was not allowed to play tennis, the compulsory game of rugger presented a particular problem to the ever sensitive young Sharp. At the age of eleven plus, both my build and temperament were hardly suited to an enthusiastic involvement in this rough, macho pastime.

'Don't put 'em down too hard,' called out the referee, an oddly humane master who, on occasions, would invite a few sixth-formers on to the field to toughen up us fragile first-formers. But young Sharp just had to find a strategy that would deceive 'em all, and afford him protection at the same time…

And why not? *I* didn't want to play their silly game. Rugger, if nothing else, is for beefy bounders – more than able to take as well as give the knocks. It was not for *me*. For who cared if my head were kicked, back broken, or fingers crushed? Ah yes, my fingers. Even then I knew my fingers would one day earn me some sort of living, however precarious. Everyone but me, it seemed, could play cricket or rugger. How many of the sods, I wondered, could play the piano? 'That's a girl's occupation', I could hear them say with sneering conviction.

There and then I made up my mind to work out my plan, and if successful, to stick to it. It turned out to be both simple and subtle, and thank The Lord, very effective. No one, I decided, could possibly know how fast or indeed how slowly my legs could move. And so, with an inbuilt braking system in my cunning brain, I would allow them to veer in the 'right' direction – well out of trouble. If the ball came my way, somehow I managed without being spotted to run to another part of the field. But never would I exaggerate what was soon to become a finely tuned process, merely in order to satisfy my craving or propensity towards the histrionic. It was all done in the best possible taste.

The plan worked beautifully, and I began to enjoy my new-found expertise in the art of deception. In the scrum I would volunteer for the job of hooker, for miraculously I could always manage to get the ball out to someone else with an efficiency which never seemed to arouse suspicion. Moreover, I rarely failed to keep the boy well down on each side of me for just that split second longer, enough to allow the danger of chasing the ball to pass. There would then be a sufficient number of bodies in front, not only to protect me, but also to do the tiresome job of tackling the other team and grounding that blasted ball over the line.

So you see, dear reader, no one would ever consider young Sharp exactly cut out for team games. He could run reasonably fast when he felt like it or by sheer necessity, and he could climb the wall-bars without too much damage, but that was about all. Now, *tennis*... Yes, you know. If only I'd been encouraged. C'est la vie.

By the time I'd reached the fifth and sixth forms, life for me had become more civilized and agreeable. Yet even here I would not entirely be let off the hook. For in the field of music in which I revelled, interference from others, little qualified, would continue to surprise and amuse me...

One unforgettable morning, a crooked but commanding finger beckoned me from the relative safety of the school library – into the judgement hall of the lobby...

'Yes, Miss Hinchley?' The Senior English Mistress, Deputy Head, and self-appointed arbiter of all things Christian stood tall, righteous, and very angry with young Sharp.

'What *were* you doing to the hymn, this morning?' School assembly, barely an hour earlier, had obviously had its affect upon this highminded yet unimaginative member within its midst. I stood back, nonplussed, for I believed I'd done a particularly good job on the piano with that damned dull hymn. But I quickly caught on to the source of Miss Hinchley's indignation.

'Oh *yes*, Miss Hinchley,' I genuinely enthused. 'I changed the harmony.'

'Changed the *harmony?*' Miss Hinchley bit back. 'You *ruined* eight hundred people's worship.'

'Oh, good,' I would like to have said. Nevertheless, I had thought it, while naturally holding my already tutored tongue. Everyone at Wanstead County High had learned to appreciate the stern eye if not the mysteries of Miss Hinchley's soul. As Master Sharp stood there, bewildered by the apparent enormity of his misdemeanour and prepared for further condemnation from Miss Hinchley's lips, his young heart leapt with glee at the stupidity and plain ignorance of certain adults around the place. He could hardly wait to relate all this to his liberal and effervescent music master.

'Those little boys at the back,' Miss Hinchley was heard to continue, 'were *craning* their necks to see what TONY SHARP was doing.

All their thoughts were turned from GOD to **TONY SHARP**.' This piece of Miss Hinchley's grand on-the-spot prosecution and assessment of little boys' thoughts, together with the magnificent emphasis upon the name TONY SHARP, was especially gratifying to the ears of its young owner who wondered whether his elation could somehow be detected by the absurd figure of authority now standing before him. Almost as though she could partially read his mind and desired, moreover, (rather sadly, it seemed) to get in on the act, she went on: 'Now, *I* can speak with some authority. I go to Wanstead House for music lessons, and the music man there is *amazed* I get all my harmonies right!'

'Gosh,' Sharp began to mouth. After all, more than one set of harmonies would stretch the imagination of some people too far. But once again, his acting ability came to his aid, and he managed to stifle an involuntary guffaw. Besides, he had begun to feel sorry for Miss Hinchley. She couldn't help it.

'Stupid cow,' said Mr Stanley, our school music master later that day, picking his nose and poring over a tattered old manuscript of 'The First Cuckoo in Spring'. Delius, apparently, was destined to be the flavour of the month, and it had to be admitted, our music master's tastes – whilst veering towards home base of Purcell but with a deep appreciation of Mr Bach – remained commendably catholic. 'Don't take any notice of *her*, boy,' he continued, dismissing Miss Hinchley from any consideration, 'what's *she* know about music?'

CHAPTER 4

Meanwhile, private piano lessons had continued apace, and I had reached Grade 8 of The Associated Board of The Royal Schools of Music. On the day of the examination I spruced myself up and jauntily walked down the road to Mr Wagstaff's house in Buckhurst Hill. His wonderful, radiant smile greeted me at the door, and I already felt good about the outcome. Not only had he been a very fine teacher of classical music but also a warm, intelligent human being with a concern for the natural nerves of his pupils. He had arranged with The Board for the examiners to hold the 'ordeals' in his own home – so that boys and girls could feel at ease on the piano they knew so well. A huge psychological advantage.

At last I entered the front room, to be introduced to Geoffrey Leeds, Doctor of Music and Organist and Choirmaster of St. James's, Paddington, where the great organist George Thalben-Ball had presided before him. Dr Leeds sported a completely bald head, immaculate pinstripe suit, stiff collar and silk tie. His face gleamed with lively, intelligent eyes which somehow expected the unexpected from his examinees. I had the distinct impression that if I'd peed on the carpet before sitting down to give a rapturous performance of Beethoven's Appassionata (should I have been able), he wouldn't have turned a hair – a serious metaphor, in his case. He would have been concentrating on the Beethoven sonata. Anyway, I had already used Mr Wagstaff's toilet, and felt pretty relaxed about things.

I can't recall what pieces I played or how I played them, but Dr Leeds seemed satisfied, and went on to ask me if I played the organ…

'Yes,' I replied brightly.

'You must come and play mine,' he ventured. Now, these were innocent days, folks, and I genuinely believed Geoffrey Leeds was referring to the big four-manual Rushworth & Draper in Paddington Parish Church.

'That's the man we want, mate,' exuded my dad when I returned home that Saturday afternoon.

'Why do you keep calling him 'mate'? His name is Tony.'

My father merely smiled in response to my mother's little dig, and continued with his assessment of the situation. 'I think it's time to move on with your organ studies.'

Even my mother agreed that wheezy old Sidney Harrington, Organist and Choirmaster of my local church and good enough to start me off, would be unable to inspire me to go further.

So a meeting with Geoffrey Leeds was arranged, and my father and I set off by Central Line tube to Lancaster Gate in The West End. We quickly located the church, and walked up the aisle towards the organ. Dr Leeds was already seated at the grand instrument, and letting rip in a stunning improvisation. As we respectfully drew near to the console, he stopped playing, and turned to us with an engaging smile.

Warmly shaking hands with us both, he invited me to play one of my party pieces. The vast organ was strange to me, but I soon selected what I judged to be suitable stops for my piece of Bach, and let go.

'I think Tony should try for an Organ Scholarship to Oxford or Cambridge, Mr Sharp.'

I could read my father's mind on hearing these words: 'This is *definitely* the man we want, mate.'

I'd even forgive his irritating habit of calling me mate, if he would support me. And that he did, and more. *No one* could wish for a more determined and generous father.

Thus plans were laid to achieve the prize of an organ scholarship, and reverse my earlier childish objection to three years at a university. Even I could see the wisdom of my father's enthusiasm.

Cambridge held a particular fascination for me, not least for the fact my father's brother, Uncle Fred, still lived there in Girton Road where I had spent six peaceful months during The Second World War, consuming good food and not a few of his delicious Victoria plums which he grew in his orchard along the road.

So after trying for several colleges, playing the chapel organs and being grilled at some distinctly odd interviews by all sorts of famous academics and musicians, I was eventually offered a place as a commoner at Queens', Cambridge, that lovely old college which backs onto and spans the river Cam so delightfully. This place was to be taken up *after* National Service.

Armed, as it were, with a commonership in my pocket, I applied for another organ scholarship the following year at Lincoln College, Oxford. But the day of the interview happened to fall on the same date as my 'A' level History Exam.

'I'm sorry, Mr Sharp. Tony will have to miss his history exam if he attends this interview.'

'But surely the papers can be sent up to Oxford? With supervision, he can sit for the exam on the same day as his interview.'

'Mr Sharp, this is highly irregular. But I can see you are a determined man. Tony is very lucky to have a father such as yourself.'

'Well?'

'I'll do my best to fix it.'

'Thank you, Mr Ingham. I know you will.'

I'm not sure Mr Ingham had at that time been privy to the bayoneting qualifications of my father's First World War years, but there must have been little doubt as to his admiration of Sharp senior. 'My word, Tony,' he confided to me the next day with a grin, 'your father will never take no for an answer. You are a lucky boy.'

The History 'A' level papers were duly sent to Lincoln College, Oxford, where I sat peacefully in the old library under the watchful but relaxed eye of a kindly old Fellow of the college.

That done, it was time to take my place in the line of hopefuls for the college organ scholarship. I availed myself of the opportunity to chat to my rivals who ranged from meek and mild 'philosophers of life' to cocky young know-alls, one of whom we all feared would be the successful candidate, not least for his early attainment of the F.R.C.O. (Fellow of The Royal College of Organists).

Yet such is the irony, perversity or justice of life – depending on the viewpoint one adopts – that the scholarship was destined to be mine.

At the time, of course, I could not know that, and I approached the examination on the organ of the college chapel with some trepidation.

My examiner was no less than the University Professor of Music himself, Jack Westrup (later to be knighted). Yet I remained determined the outcome, whichever way it went, would not really matter. The Cambridge place helped me to relax a little, and I quickly learned to appreciate the penetrating, intelligent face of Jack Westrup with his naughty eyes and subtle humour.

The chapel organ at that time – mid 50s – must have been the smallest instrument the illustrious firm of Harrison & Harrison had ever built: just two manuals, very few stops, and only one 16 foot stop for the pedals. But it possessed a sweet tone, and I soldiered on... I cannot recall what pieces I played, but when it came to the extemporization, I let go a trifle more, and Jack Westrup, thank The Lord, made a timely interjection: 'I'm sorry to stop you there, just as you were about to go into a six-part fugue.' Fat chance of *that,* I thought, grateful for the interruption.

I returned home to London, convinced I had not done well enough to clinch the scholarship, despite the pleasant atmosphere pervading the interviews.

'Never mind, Tony. You still have the place at Cambridge.'

'It's early days,' added my father. 'Let's wait and see.' And we all sat down to a delicious meal of grilled fresh herrings with big roes, caught in the rich fishing waters which still surrounded

The British Isles – long before they were signed away in 1972 by a Conservative Prime Minister as the price for entry into the EC the following year. How the Continentals must have rubbed their hands with glee and disbelief that the British would ever do such a thing. Back in the 50s, it would have been an inconceivable act of irresponsibility and shame.

CHAPTER 5

'Wake up, mate. Listen to this.' My father proudly pushed out his chest, and stood back at the foot of my bed to read the telegram, three short weeks after the interviews at Oxford... CONGRATULATIONS.

I had been offered an Organ Scholarship at Lincoln College, to be taken up *before* National Service, and on condition I passed 'O' level Latin. 'So, get that Latin, mate.'

I had no time to waste. My father was at it again, cajoling and encouraging my Headmaster to push me in attaining my Latin. Considered too dim to tackle the subject in my second year at school, the scene had dramatically changed by the time I'd reached the sixth. With the incentive of an Organ Scholarship at Oxford on a plate, and a fraction more maturity about me, I eagerly took up the challenge and did the thing from scratch in six months. In addition to Arthur Ingham himself, the delightful and appropriately named Mr Quick was promptly assigned to give me individual lessons. He certainly held his name intact, and I grew to enjoy a 'dead' language from which so many living tongues derive. The study also stirred in me a new interest in my own language. How otherwise, for instance, would I ever have known the word 'procrastinate' to arise so conveniently from Latin? PRO=UNTIL or FOR. CRAS=TOMORROW… And how was I to know, until much later, that some enterprising Cockney would enunciate such an unlikely word, just so he could wedge the Chaucerian 'fuck' in the middle? PROCRASTIFUCKIN'ATE, let's face it, is quite impressive, quite an achievement for a so-called 'deprived', unsophisticated bloke.

And so, with 'O' level Latin in the bag, together with the other exam results, and the civilized pleasure of an amusing interview with Professor Westrup, not to mention the meeting with the newly appointed Rector of Lincoln College, Dr Oakshott (ex-Headmaster of Winchester and one of the most agreeable and non-stuffy human beings anyone could encounter), I went up to Oxford.

Happily, my father loaded the trunk into the pull-down boot of his Ford Popular, though how it ever achieved such an accolade, God alone knew. With its mournful face, featuring a long upright radiator reminding one of a lone thin thermometer without the colouring or hope of better things to come, and piggy little headlamps with barely enough light to pick out a couple of cat's-eyes, it braved the highways of England. When the wind blew, it blew with it. Loaded up, one had to wait for the wind to be kind in order to change course.

Yet somehow my father managed. He was a fighter, after all... We broke the journey on the old A40 at High Wycombe, and downed a pint apiece at The Swan, and continued the drive to Oxford, he full of pride and goodwill, I not a little apprehensive and nervous of much that might be expected of me.

Dumping the luggage in the rooms of my college, he took me out to a fine old inn... I was treated to my first 'blue' steak. I have since grown to enjoy a good blue, but in those days a rare steak with blood running out suited me just fine. For as a lover of good food himself, my father was wont to cook me superb breakfasts before I took Communion as a young boy at the local church. The Rector of the parish, as was only to be expected, had indicated the idea was to *fast* before the service – as an act of reverence, contrition and identification with The Last Supper. Serious enough...

'However,' said The Rector sympathetically, 'if you are likely to faint without food, for goodness sake have something.'

Something, as far as my father was concerned, would consist of a perfect, rare point end Scotch rump, and French fries with Colman's mustard. Or to ring the changes, he'd cook me a delicious halibut steak. What fish. I've hardly tasted such halibut since those halcyon days. Then on other occasions he'd come up with two large scallops in their shells: orgasmically wonderful. The scallops, by the way, were merely considered an hors-d'oeuvre by my father to the main course of the halibut (deep fried in best quality oil) or that rump, a beautiful point end piece near the fillet, but with so much more flavour. My mouth waters with the memory… Stop talking about food, Sharp… Sorry, but I can't help the Jewish and French blood coursing through my 'British' veins. Besides, in those days, there appeared not the slightest hint of gout about my person, and I innocently relegated such a consideration to figures of eighteenth and nineteenth century cartoon fun. It was nothing to do with me. Oh, the confidence of youth!

After a splendid lunch, we returned to my rooms in the college, and with a few words of encouragement and best wishes from my father, we parted with a hug and kiss, and promise on both sides to write.

When my father had gone I made a large pot of tea, and treated myself to fulsome masturbation in the empty tea carton. It was hardly an expression of protest, and certainly no disrespect to Typhoo tea: more a sense of mad liberation. How was I to know until later that Dudley Moore with whom I'd share tutorials would soon be wanking himself silly, every spare minute of the day? 'I just can't stop,' he'd say, as I got to know him. A few years later, as all the world appears to know, this activity would seem paltry stuff indeed – compared to his exploits with some of the most beautiful women on earth. I loved him, bless his soul. As far as I'm concerned, he never changed (even when he became rich and famous) from that thoughtful, lost boy character to whom music and comedy came so naturally and brilliantly. A rare talent indeed.

It was time to attend my first tutorial. I knocked on the door of Dr Bernard Rose's quarters. 'Come in,' he shouted without hesitation. As I entered his elegant rooms in The Queen's College, his cheery and decidedly military grin greeted me, together with a far less military but exceedingly sensitive and warm smile from my fellow student, 'cuddly' Dudley Moore, who'd be my partner in those weekly tutorials for the next three years. Between us we would entertain Dr Rose to such an extent that he always thought of us as a double act. In fact, he once suggested I should give up music and go on the stage. Maybe he had a point. But the irony was that Dudley would become the star of stage and screen and never neglect his music whilst Sharp would fumble around, clutching at straws, and failing to concentrate and capitalize on his successes and opportunities. C'est la vie.

My other tutor, for the study of the history of music, was a delightful elderly Fellow of my own college, Lincoln, an erudite Austrian who took rooms in the front quadrangle but who also occupied a fine eighteenth-century house in Woodstock Road. His study on the first floor where he held his tutorials was filled with books from floor to ceiling, and he relished relating tit-bits of gossip about other composers and musicians... I didn't care for Egon Wellesz's music, I confess, but I loved his stories...

'Rubbra was *furious*,' he exploded with apparent authority one memorable morning. 'Malcolm Sargent came to the first rehearsal without having *looked* at the score.' Wellesz was referring to Edmund Rubbra's Sixth Symphony which I'd heard on the radio, direct from a Promenade Concert at The Royal Albert Hall in London.

Later in the week I decided to tackle Rubbra about this. After all, he was our lecturer for that week at The Music Faculty in Hollywell. Strolling casually up to him after his lecture, I said I'd heard through the grapevine he had not been too pleased with the interpretation of his new symphony at the hands of the famous conductor, nicknamed 'Flash Harry' at the time. 'Oh, I don't know,' smiled Rubbra sweetly. 'It wasn't too bad.' A euphemism, perhaps, for a cock-up in his eyes? Or a generous comment on a sub-standard performance? Maybe he knew the general public would barely notice the difference. Modern music, after all, can easily deceive the uninitiated, and blur the lines of 'right' and 'wrong'. For to quote Rubbra's own words to me with his enigmatic smile: "There is no such thing as a discord; only *tensions* of sound."

I had been put in my place yet again.

CHAPTER 6

And talking of blurring the lines, I recall with pleasure and nostalgia the occasion of the first rehearsal of Stravinsky's 'Symphony of Psalms' by The Bach Choir of Oxford. I had joined as an innocent member of the choir, both for fun and perhaps a further insight into a wider range of music than the period of my chosen study.

Now, this was to be a classic scene for all time as Dr H.K.Andrews, Oxford lecturer, Organist and Master of the Choristers of New College, and a world authority on sixteenth century English church music, presided over this rehearsal of Stravinsky's masterpiece while Thomas Armstrong, The Bach Choir's regular conductor, languished in his sick-bed at home. Unlike Dr Armstrong (later Sir Thomas), Dr Andrews had little time for modern music, and made no attempt to hide the fact. 1500 to the 1620s, perhaps 1656 at a push with the death of Thomas Tomkins, would remain his 'patch'. And now that he'd been obliged to help out in a rehearsal, moreover of a seemingly discordant new work (it has since become a modern classic, of course, and one of my personal favourites), he decided he'd extract a bit of fun from the ordeal...

'Please, Dr Andrews.' The rehearsal had already ground to a halt. A lone hand raised itself from the body of the choir. 'I've got F sharp in my score in the alto section.'

'Oh, *I* have F double sharp,' shouted another confident lady.

'What about my B flat as opposed to my neighbour's B natural in the basses?' added a local wit.

'Stravinsky doesn't seem to know what he wants, himself,' grunted Dr Andrews with a much appreciated, wicked grin.

Several members of the choir, including myself, had a few pages stuck together in our new austerity copies, so that it was difficult to see what Stravinsky had indeed intended.

And Dr Andrews had clearly had enough nonsense for the night. 'Oh, *leave* it,' he continued in his dry tone. 'I dare say it'll *all* blend in.'

Uncontrolled laughter erupted from the whole choir, and it was a job to get the rehearsal going again. Serious work had obviously been written off, and Thomas Armstrong was encouraged by the powers that be to recoup from his illness at a smart pace.

On another occasion during one of Dr Andrews's casual lectures to us 'Freshmen' – in the form of a discussion with him as arbiter – the talk veered to the subject of Baroque organs (European church organs of the seventeenth and eighteenth centuries), often copied in the twentieth century by British organ builders in response to the demands of many international recitalists, ever anxious to produce authentic interpretations of baroque music…

'What is your opinion of these instruments, Dr Andrews?' asked one bright student, hoping perhaps to catch his man out.

With a wonderful, cynical snarl, the great man looked his questioner full in the face:

'I like my music in *one key at a time*, if you don't mind.' The rest of us burst out laughing. It was obvious the prominent harmonics of many of the stops on Baroque organs offended a very particular academic. Physically, he resembled John Foster Dulles, the American Secretary of State serving President Eisenhower, and was as hard to move as his physical counterpart…

For when at last he took his final breath, he refused to leave this world without making the point. This was some time later, when I had been appointed University Organist at Oxford, a post I held for two stressful years, ending them with a spectacular crash in my new Mini Cooper on the old A40. The car was a write-off, but I survived, and after being patched up in The Radcliffe

Infirmary, they brought me home to my house in Witney. The driver of the ambulance chatted away to me on the journey…

'What d'you do for a living?' he asked in the front cab where I sat with him, nursing my wounds. When I told him about my work and background he immediately retorted: 'Ah well, you must have known Dr Andrews.'

'I certainly did,' I answered with a grin. But the ambulance man's smile widened further. 'I helped to bring the body down from the organ loft, you know. Bloody heavy man, he was. And all those steps. It took us ages.'

Dr H.K.Andrews had indeed died on the job, in the musical sense, you understand. He had been playing at the opening ceremony of the re-built organ of Trinity College, Oxford. When it came to the 150th psalm, he let go and began to enjoy himself. With the instrument at full stretch in The Gloria, he promptly died, dropping dramatically on to the keys of the Great Organ.

Now, Dr Andrews might never have been regarded as the finest of organists at Oxford (and there had been some very fine exponents over the years), but this was going too far. As his considerable body flopped down and splayed itself across the manuals, an inordinate number of keys were unavoidably held down – all continuing to sound in an excruciating cacophony. Nothing Stravinsky had ever written could equal this. A suddenly horrified congregation was treated to a final Andrewism, ironically in all the keys at the same time.

What a way to go; parallel, perhaps, to Tommy Cooper during his last stage act. Maybe even more dramatic. And almost as unnerving as 'dying on the job' with the wife. Lovely for the man. Not so lovely for the wife, I should think. "Till death us do part" in these circumstances would take even the imaginative by surprise, and parting could hardly be described as such sweet sorrow.

CHAPTER 7

The three years at Oxford raced by, leaving me wondering what the hell I should do.

'Well, you'll have to go into teaching, mate.' My father still found it hard to drop the 'mate' bit. But he remained a good father, and for ever supportive. Little could he conceive, of course, that I would leave the teaching profession so soon in the late 60s and proceed to muck up my life, making a fool of myself in clubs, pubs and low dives. By that time, he would be dead, God rest his soul. Besides, among the rough jobs I would learn a little more about life as it is, rather than what my father wished it to be for me. I would also chalk up some classy work, both solo and with named artists; and a fair amount of gigs abroad would provide me unlimited material for all sorts of off-beat novels, should I ever dare to publish them. In any case, life to my mind will always be stranger than the strangest of fiction.

So, in the late 50s I duly clocked in as a full-time student at The University of London for a one-year course towards a teaching diploma. At least it might keep my father off my back a while longer, I believed. And it was there, at The Institute of Education that I met a charming and extremely lively Welshman by the name of Kenneth Bowen. He possessed a fine tenor voice and in due course he'd become a top-class lieder and oratorio soloist, performing all over the world in a career that afforded him a beautiful house in Hampstead – with a Steinway grand in one room, and a Bechstein in another. Like his sons who followed him, he went up to Cambridge for his degree, Ken as a choral scholar at St. John's College. His Welshness remained merely a springboard from which he could survey and taste the world. His was an open mind, and he possessed more than a touch of Harry Secombe's goonery.

Perhaps it was Goonery that led him to agree to be tenor soloist in The Messiah at St. Andrew's, Plaistow – a large church situated near a sewer. Moreover, Ken did it all for five pounds, Sterling. Not much for such a fine performance, even in 1958. But there it was. He seemed glad of the experience with a fellow madman, yours truly on harpsichord, while Eric Stanley (my old music master at Wanstead County High School, and another mad but inspiring musician) conducted the choir and orchestra. Plaistow, that evening, had a rare treat bestowed upon it. Not a niff could be detected from the nearby sewer, since all minds, it seemed, were concentrated upon the performance. St. Andrew's was a large church with acoustics which lent themselves to fine choral and orchestral music. Moreover, it was an establishment where I could let go and throw off some of the preciousness acquired at Oxford.

'I don't like your being at Plaistow, Tony.' My father for once had decided to drop the 'mate', clean up his grammar, and distance himself from my attempt, in his eyes, to 'slum it'... But soon after coming down from Oxford I had applied for a post as Organist and Choirmaster, and advertised in 'The Church Times'. The Rev. Eric Shipman phoned me and said he appreciated my words 'Ambitious young graduate seeks interesting post...', but went on to assure me that, nearby sewer aside, I should indeed find the post interesting.

I served five very happy years at St. Andrew's among the good old Cockneys and real people. I also met some outstanding and individual clergy whose philosophy and outlook on life would, of course, no longer shock the general public. I can hardly forget one young curate who might well have been happier in a silent order. He sported a gammy leg as a result of falling off the back of a bus – not after helping a damsel in distress: his story.

'There's nothing I hate more than the sound of the human voice,' he droned one sunny afternoon, after officiating at a wedding. Needless to say, his own voice could depress the most sympathetic and patient of his congregation (and often did), and he avoided all musical vocalizing as much as possible. Very wise.

David Shepherd was a different kettle of fish. He ran a Boys' Club at that time – The Mayflower, Canning Town, but often officiated at weddings in St. Andrew's. A fine and famous cricketer with an engaging personality who went on to grander things as Bishop of Liverpool, he impressed most people with his physique and open countenance.

Sir Ian Horobin ran the rival establishment, Fairburn Boys' Club in Plaistow. Some of the boys were treated to a ride in his Rolls Royce and other tit bits in return for a few sexual favours, the latter activity inevitably frowned upon by the authorities, but also by the Rev. Eric Shipman who was eager to have Sir Ian's job, without the sex. Such is human nature, folks.

Robert Coogan was another young, talented curate with a highly developed sense of humour. Of Irish stock, he had lived in Tasmania with his parents, and one day wrote to Eric Shipman to inform him: 'I'm coming to England. I think England *needs* me.' He possessed a first-rate intellect, and could easily have risen to a Bishopric, yet after a stint as vicar of a parish in North Woolwich he landed himself a cushy number as Rural Dean of Hampstead. The position suited him admirably where his taste and knowledge of antiques, off-beat humour, life-style, and superior manners were appreciated by some and decently ignored by others. Hampstead is Hampstead.

Yet before I made my own move to The West End to 'further' my career and widen those horizons a shade, I instinctively felt there was still more to savour and pack away in my memory box. Around March and April, for instance, there were countless weddings at St. Andrew's which required an organist to jolly things up. The average on Saturdays, I suppose, was about ten, but I do remember playing *sixteen* in one day, and falling off the organ stool with a fairly sore bottom but with a big enough pay packet for a bloody good meal and piss-up with some friends. Not that the money was anything to go wild about, by today's standards. One has to remember this was the late 50s. I was awarded, in fact, the then handsome sum of one and a half guineas a shot... And talking of 'shot-gun' weddings, how could I ever forget them? The bride, bless her, would unashamedly push out her already sizeable stomach and pronounce her love for her spouse who in turn would barely control his nervousness and embarrassment in the presence of the vicar, Eric Shipman, whose never-ending smile would oversee the proceedings and make everything seem all right.

But on another occasion, we were warned there might be some trouble with the bride's former boyfriend. It had soon become obvious he was a very determined young man who would try to stop the wedding in dramatic form. Well, determined he might be: so was our vicar. He made sure *all* the doors of the church were firmly locked. And as the angry young man proceeded to shake and bang away, the service was rushed through, the couple pronounced man and wife, and the young guy informed of the fait accompli.

CHAPTER 8

Young, ambitious and keen as I still was, I harboured hopes that I could persuade the Rev. Eric Shipman that we needed a complete rebuild of the organ in St. Andrew's, Plaistow. I'd had enough, frankly, of its wheezing, puffing and blowing, squeaks, bangs and other malfunctions – with precious little compensation in the form of musical sounds to which I'd aspired. There comes a time, I reminded him, when all things must pass, and much to my surprise, he agreed. So plans were drawn up and specifications submitted by various British organ builders, most of whom had succumbed to the new wave of demands from top organists for a more authentic tone and action to their chosen instrument. For so long the cathedral organs of England had celebrated a glorious mish-mash of orchestral sounds – entirely suited, it was believed, to the confident, empirical romanticism of the Victorian era. Why should England be influenced by those darned foreigners?

But times were a-changing. Scholarship was pointing the way. Bach must sound like Bach intended. There were to be no more excuses.

It was to The Continent that organ recitalists looked from the 1950s onwards. Ralph Downes, organist of Brompton Oratory, famously led the way with his design of the magnificent organ in The Royal Festival Hall, opened in 1951 as part of The Festival of Britain celebrations. The esteemed firm of Harrison & Harrison clinched the contract for this instrument, but there were several other firms in serious competition and eager to get in on the current rage. Of these I personally found the directors of Walker Organs most helpful in my searches. In fact, they took me to many locations where they had installed one of their 'Baroque' efforts… The organ of Brompton Oratory impressed me the most. It had, of course, also been designed by Ralph Downes and exhibited a sparkling array of colours, perfectly matched to the lively acoustics of the building. Together with its beautifully weighted tracker action, the organ proved a delight to play. I was hooked.

Accordingly, in order to gain more experience and clarify my ideas for a re-build of St. Andrew's organ, I took a trip to The Continent in the summer of 1959. The North Sea remained calm, for a change – incredibly like a millpond, in fact, and I thanked God for deliverance from the slightest hint of sea-sickness. On board ship, destined for Copenhagen, sat my little Austin A35 plus two other guys, Barry Paine (who later worked for the BBC) and Colin Liebenrood. Barry would take the magnificent black and white pictures of the organs I would record, and Colin would be our 'recording engineer'.

He did a splendid job with his Revox machine, and I was able to let myself go on the organ of Holmens Kirche, Copenhagen, with Bach's famous Toccata and Fugue in D minor. But my real favourite instrument of the trip was to be the Great Organ of St. Laurenskerk in Alkmaar, Holland. The history of this magnificent organ stretches back centuries, and the instrument is one of the best maintained in the whole of the Netherlands. It is a thrill to play: powerful, full of character and with brilliant mixtures, the harmonics of which might well have endangered the peaceful grave of our old friend Dr H.K. Andrews, were he not (I hope) so interestingly occupied 'on the other side'.

I returned to England, full of joy and confidence, believing I would realize my dream of a fine organ for St. Andrews. Stupidly, however, I opened my big mouth too soon and informed The Rev. Eric Shipman that Walkers were now producing a

'Positive' organ – a scaled-down two manual, cheap job for fifteen hundred pounds: a slight difference, it had to be admitted, to ten thousand pounds. 'We'll have the 'The Positive', Tony,' he quickly decided. 'We really don't have the money for your grand scheme.'

Bugger it. I'd fouled up again. My own enemy I might forever be. In fact, looking back on my life, there have been precious few sensible decisions taken. Maybe I really *am* a masochist and it's part of my nature or at best an attempt to see what happens as a result of a wrong turning. 'How stupid can you be?' I hear some of you cry. You may well be right. But I have long believed in the necessity of Ying and Yang, and I take pleasure in the ebb and flow of positive and negative: good copy for my books, perhaps. But is there really any point, you may ask, in being so negative when life itself will surely dish out enough blows without one adding fuel to the process?

But in the same year of 1959, I registered as a full-time student at Trinity College of Music, London, then situated in Mandeville Place, W1. Valda Aveling was my harpsichord teacher, and Arnold Cooke my tutor in composition. I had been attracted to Trinity College, not least for the fact that it was the only college at that time to offer harpsichord lessons, leading to diplomas in the subject. But I also knew Arnold Cooke had been a pupil of Paul Hindemith whose music I was mad keen on – much to the chagrin of my father who had struggled to appreciate my weird tastes and individualism. Thank Heavens he was intelligent enough to realize I was past redemption.

In order to bring in a few pennies, I got a part-time job, teaching little boys the piano in a Preparatory School – St. Alban's, Woodford Green, Essex. It was my first teaching job, and opened my eyes to the fact there is no way one can make "a silk purse out of a sow's ear". And in a subject like music, talent is either there or it isn't. Nevertheless, it remains a joy to see even a smidgen of progress, particularly when a youngster has worked for it.

A stone's throw from this little school was a car showroom, featuring new Austins, and in 1960 there sat the new Austin Healey Sprite – 'frog-eyed' in stark white with red interior. It was to be my first sports car. The salesman tried to persuade me to buy a new Austin Healey 3000 which sat behind the Sprite. It had been a cancelled order, so he said I could have it for nine hundred pounds. But the difference between six hundred and forty and nine hundred was a lot of money in those days, especially for a supposedly penniless teacher. So I played safe, and went for the Sprite…

My father put his glasses on to give the car a thorough going over. He grimaced at the small size and likelihood of a short life in my hands (the Frog-Eyed Sprite is a collector's piece now, of course), but in time he began to realize its good qualities and uniqueness. Not only that, but he kindly bought my Austin A35…

'But you can buy a brand new one for that money, dad.'

'No, Tony, I like your one. It'll do for me.'

What luck, I thought. I hope the A35 won't give him any trouble. But my father seemed pleased and could often be seen smiling to himself as he tried to negotiate a three-point turn in our road – after he'd returned from a business/drinking session with some of his navy pals. The three-point turn, by the way, sometimes became a five, six or even seven-point operation for good measure, before the car came safely to rest at its berth by the kerb outside our house. Those were the days, of course, before the strict drink and drive laws, rightly imposed upon us all across the UK.

1961 brought further changes to stimulate the little grey cells of my mind. I was appointed Head of the Music Department at The Royal Liberty School, Gidea Park in Essex. I remember working hard and fast to produce my first concert with the school orchestra and choir... And as the build-up to 'Zadok The Priest' rose in orchestral crescendo, the choir prepared to reach for the sky and attack those magical chords with gleeful enthusiasm, pinning the audience to their seats in unexpected terror: they had never known their young sons to sing with such vigour... But despite the obvious success of the concert and the praises of The Headmaster ("Tony Sharp has fire in his belly" he was heard to remark) I still did not achieve a proper music room in which to conduct lessons. The Head, in fact, appeared to enjoy my playing one of the upright pianos while a few boys wheeled the damned thing along the corridors. It was Sharp's way of rubbing it in that we needed a separate room. 'You can truly consider yourself peripatetic', The Head merely quipped from the side of his mouth one day, and nonchalantly walked on.

During the summer of that year, I travelled to Germany and Austria with a friend and fellow teacher, Ian Lister. Ian spoke fluent German with a regional accent, and he had made many German friends over the years. Yet this was but sixteen years after the end of the war, and we stayed in an elegant German house in the little German hamlet of Bodenfelde. The Head of the household had been in the Luftwaffe. I sat right next to him as we spooned our first course of Russian goulash that night. 'I bombed your country *eighteen* times,' he said without hesitation. 'Thank you very much,' I said under my breath, for the latter, I must admit, had been suddenly taken away from me. 'When are you coming over again?' I wanted to add cynically as I struggled to recover, but he quickly followed up with: 'No, Tony. It was *terrible*. We *had* to do it, or The Gestapo would shoot us.' This man, sixteen years after the war, still displayed a nervous twitch when he drove his Mercedes. He kept looking down as if he were pressing the bomb release button. But now it was peacetime. He got his employees to clean my little English car before they went back to work in the factory, making cheese. The man not only owned the factory, but had made all the machines himself. He had fathered eleven children, and he and his wife appeared reasonably content with the way life had turned out for them. The large house overlooked a wide, deep gorge at the bottom of which flowed the River Weser (Pied Piper of Hamelin fame). Years later in Spain, I met a German ex-pat who had delivered bread to that very factory in Bodenfelde when he was a boy. What a small world.

Two other events stick out in my mind in that year of 1961: the first was the loan of a beautiful eighteenth century two-manual harpsichord – made in 1777 in London by the harpsichord maker Kirckman – and loaned to me by the late Tom Goff, whose own instruments displayed, in my opinion, the most gorgeous and refined sounds that could be emitted from a plucked string keyboard. Most of us are well aware of the famous Sir Thomas Beecham quip about the harpsichord sounding "like two skeletons copulating on a tin roof ". Well, Tom Goff's instruments were anything but that.

Moreover, he would later lend me one for my Purcell Room recitals and BBC Late Night Line Ups... The second occurrence of '61 was the achievement of the F.T.C.L. (Fellow of Trinity College, London), the first person in the world, I was told, to be awarded this in harpsichord playing. And to top it all, so to speak, I received my prize from the hands of Sir John Barbirolli, that great and much-loved conductor of The Hallé Orchestra: it was a beautifully bound and illustrated hardback on eighteenth century harpsichords, including the very one Tom had loaned me.

A few years later, he decided to make me a gift of the Kirckman. Only a mad aristocrat would do such a thing for an impecunious musician. But then, Tom Goff *had* entered this world via a long line of Georges. Mistressess were the norm, in those days, and there was no such thing as a gross, frenetic media, poking its nose into Royal matters. Not that Tom ever worried much about the modern world, God rest his soul.

CHAPTER 9

1962 saw the sudden death of my father, who had been rushed to hospital one bitter morning, after he had collapsed in the bathroom while shaving. He died before they could operate, having been left on the stretcher in a cold corridor for too long. We knew he had symptoms of arterial cirrhosis for the last two years of his life, but the suddenness of his death, nevertheless, was a shock. Mind you, he had often said he would die "in harness", and perhaps he would not have been happy, mooching around the house in slippers. This was hardly his style.

I took two weeks off duty in order to do the Probate and comfort my mother. I was then driving my second Austin Healey Sprite (first of the square models), but my mother kept sliding under the dash-board as she attempted to sit in the passenger seat. 'Oh, bloody silly car, Tony. Why don't you get one people can sit in? I'll help you out with the money.'

Needless to say, we found ourselves ogling the brand new model of a flashy-looking Sunbeam Rapier in a local showroom. 'Would you like that, Tony?' My mother was a wonderful temptress. 'Certainly I would, mum. But I think you should look after what little money you have. Thanks for the offer, but I think I'll buy a nice second-hand, comfortable car from The Mill Garage...´ There I spotted a 1957 MG ZB in dark, highly polished red with biscuit leather interior, *and*, of course, a real polished walnut dash and door surrounds... The glove box on the front passenger side clicked with gentle precision, and the little octagonal clock in the roof lining above the windscreen ticked with maddening refinement. I made a cruel habit of teasing a vicar friend with the class concept. 'Oh, you *wretch*', he would squeak with an appreciative grin.

The following year I made a move to Chingford County High, then a nice little mixed grammar school of around three hundred and fifty pupils. But it would not be long before it slid into a badly organized Comprehensive which even some of the notorious 'reds' on the staff would come to loathe.

In the same year of 1963, The West End beckoned, landing me the job as Organist and Choirmaster of St.Peter's Church, Cranley Gardens, SW7, a post once occupied by Arthur Sullivan of light opera fame. For me, it would certainly be a congenial tenure – with a professional choir to conduct and the support and friendship of an intelligent, humorous vicar with whom I could work in an atmosphere of consummate ease.

The Reverend Cyril Dams had, for twelve years, enjoyed himself as Precentor of Westminster Abbey, officiating at many a grand occasion, not least The Coronation of Her Majesty, Queen Elizabeth in 1953. But now he had been put out to grass… 'I dare say I could have stayed if I'd dug my toes in,' he confessed to me at our first meeting, held in his rooms in Dean's Yard, Westminster. What a nice, honest, open man, I thought then. And time would prove me right in my assessment.

I'd like to think my musical contribution to the services of St. Peter's did not disappoint him too much. But if it ever did, he would never show such sentiment. In fact, when after two years I made yet another move, this time to return to Oxford as University Organist, he pulled me aside to whisper: 'If you change your mind, Tony, I want you to know I'd be very happy for you to stay'. If only I'd taken up his offer. But everything is easy with hindsight…

He was a lovely, human man with a wicked sense of humour. I recall so well his bold announcement to a confused group of elderly folk at his first parish meeting. He had got up on to the platform and faced them with his special, enigmatic smile… 'I hope you will forgive my absence for the next half hour,' he calmly stated, 'but the organist and I have a predilection for 'Steptoe & Son'.' And off we both trotted to watch TV in the vicarage next door.

How, too, could I ever forget his unusual sermon (unique in the world, I'd say) one sunny Sunday morning on the humour of Jesus Christ? Cyril Dams looked kindly upon his congregation of six ladies in the front pews of St. Peter's, built to accommodate well over a thousand souls, and ploughed on regardless. He suggested Christ laughed so much and so often that The Scriptures never bothered to report this side of his character. The old ladies gazed up into their vicar's face and wondered what the hell he was talking about. My choir and I giggled with almost surreal amusement and delight. How lucky we all were to be spared the interminable spoutings of a stuffy, boring prig. *Our* vicar was a one-off - a highly intelligent, open-minded, happy human being.

And then in 1964, he asked me if I'd like to give an organ recital in Westminster Abbey, as part of the summer series. I would have ample time to practice in the evenings, and he would do his best to ensure I'd have a healthily large audience to attend the recital. Wow. How could I resist?

Now, this was all before my days of jazzing things up, folks, although I suspect Cyril Dams had his suspicions. Anyway, I promised him I would keep the programme on classical lines, barring the odd chance of a slight aberration in the form of a work by Sharp. Cyril Dams looked at me with interest. 'Seriously,' I assured him, 'it's merely a trifle energetic and in the style, somewhat, of Paul Hindemith.' He grimaced for a while and then softened his expression into the smile I knew well.

So, into the Abbey I would slip at night, not knowing whose ghost I would meet before I'd reached the vast organ loft. And *who* would be sitting on the organ stool when I got there? Now this was many years before I'd published my first book called 'The Guv'nor' – in the course of which God, in the guise of Sammy Davis, Junior, appears sitting at the organ of King's College Chapel, Cambridge. But the organ loft of Westminster Abbey can accommodate a great body of performers. Was it not possible…? Shut up, Sharp. Well, I reached the loft without drama, thanked God for sparing me a jolt, and began my practice. After that, subsequent nights held little fear for me, and then… the day arrived.

With steadied nerves, I climbed the steps to the organ loft. At my side walked a pretty, young Welsh singer, who, I suspect, was a little in love with me at the time. She would turn the pages of my music and help to alleviate my isolation in the organ loft. With my mother downstairs in the stalls, and, nearby, my harpsichord teacher, Valda Aveling, together with my friend Tom Goff, I remained determined not only to do justice to the Abbey organ but also to let go and enjoy the whole experience.

Dismissing from my mind the horrors of all that could easily go wrong while playing such a powerful instrument in so famous a church as this where great history is made and recorded and so many monarchs have been crowned, I commended my soul to God and dug in... And before I knew it, the recital was over, and I thanked Heaven there had been no mishap or embarrassing moment of reckoning, save perhaps for my own work during which I let fly. After all, I'd written the damned piece. I could interpret it as I saw fit.

'Did you enjoy it, mum?' I could see my mother was anxious to commend me but balance things up, at the same time.

'Yes, Tony,' she said with an intimate smile. 'I think you played a little bit *too* loud, there,' she smartly added. Honest to the last, bless her. Her remark put everything in perspective, and served to humble me a shade. Yet I received enough informed congratulations from those in the know to keep me happy for the rest of the day. Oh, the ego of a musician. Nevertheless, for once I was pleased with my own performance, and most certainly grateful for not playing any bum notes on the pedals when pulling the 32 foot Ophicleide stop. These pipes release a pretty distinctive farting sound, if nothing else. As for the Bach, Buxtehude and César Franck, my audience seemed satisfied and therefore, I think, accepted the madness of my own work with good grace…

'We'd know it was you, Tony, even without the programme in our hands.' An apt remark, uttered by a close friend without malice and with not a little love.

CHAPTER 10

The return to Oxford in 1965 marked an important pivotal change in my life, and would affect other loved ones for ever.

As the letter of invitation stood open in my 'lucky' hands, a myriad of emotions and considerations struggled for priority. Was it time to leave home and cut the umbilical cord, only to attach myself to the memory of my late father? How proud he would be to know I had clinched the job as University Organist. Moreover, I remember sitting in the gallery of St. Mary the Virgin as a student, looking across to the organ case in the middle of the church and musing: 'I'd like to be organist here, one day.' Ten years later, the job would be mine.

'You'll miss your professional choir, won't you?' asked Dr Lumsden (later Sir David) at the interview. Should I take the job, and to hell with the consequences and regrets? Perhaps I could learn something. For on paper, the prospects looked reasonable enough: University Organist, responsible for the services of St. Mary the Virgin, to play for all official city functions, held in the church; Head of Music at Burford Grammar School (but already a sprawling Comprehensive); the 'incentive' of some teaching at The Faculty of Music (this never materialized), and... What the devil had I done?

With the very first service barely over, the still youthful Tony Sharp was treated to a visitation in the organ-loft from his immediate employer: 'I *will* not have the services of God *ruined*,' screamed the ugly distorted mouth. I leant back on the organ stool, and turned to face the mouth. Surely my days of early indiscretions were over? Or could it be my eyes and ears were already beginning to pack up with the strain of life as it was, rather than as I'd like it to be? For before me, in the 'sanctity' of the organ-loft, stood a very irate and red-faced vicar. In fact, the man's qualifications were considered by some to have been superior to those of a mere vicar: he was The Rural Dean of Oxford, no less. And who better than the local poet and author of 'ME and ME ALONE' to put Sharp in his place?

A somewhat grotesque and twisted vision of Miss Hinchley came flooding back into my mind. For whereas that particular incident – so many years before as a schoolboy – had been fun, *this*, most certainly, was not. My job, it appeared, was at stake; and after only one day.

As the vicar stormed off, stomping down the hard stone steps – a 'redneck' in rampant, unabated anger – I began to wonder how and why on earth I'd really chosen to leave London. The only damage, to my mind, done to this particular service of God (should HE have been in the least interested) was that one of the dullest of all the tunes penned in The English Hymnal (and it has to be said: there are quite a number) had either been omitted altogether or played *after* instead of *before* the final prayer. Looking back on that incident, I wished I'd substituted the dreary hymn with a spirited version of 'Take the 'A' Train', and had done with it. At least I could have gone out in rapid and totally satisfying disgrace, and returned to London a penniless yet happy man.

But the torture was destined to continue. There were a few light reliefs – in the form of some good food and a drink or two, but in the main my unhappiness intensified. It was as though the visitation in the loft pervaded the next two years. Even the change of car, from an MGB (which I'd purchased, part-exchanging the MG ZB saloon) to a brand new Mini Cooper, had the jinx all over it. I had wanted a red one with white top, but a green with white top was the only one available at the time from my 'friendly' garage in Ilford who took the MGB off my hands... The Mini Cooper of today is a very different animal: strong, well-built and well-finished. The 60s Coopers, in my opinion, were thrown together.

Mine had white paint already pealing off its roof. At 2,000 miles, the windscreen shattered in front of me while travelling along a country lane. At 4,000 miles, I headed straight for an almighty crash on the old A40, driving back to London one weekend. The car was a write-off, and I still bear the scars of the accident today.

Yet a good lesson was learned from this: never assume anyone will do what you expect him to do. Imagine you have eyes at the back of your head, too… The practical and artistic spin-offs from the accident pleased me more. I was awarded two weeks break from school teaching during which time I wrote my first jazz pieces for harpsichord. Tom Goff agreed I should house the Kirckman in my new home in Witney. There it sat, in the L-shaped sitting-room, and while nursing internal bruises and leg wounds, and growing a hideous beard in order to cover the stitching on my chin, I allowed my fingers to wander over the keys and do what they willed. A set of pieces, specifically for the harpsichord, ensued which would result in a Purcell Room recital in London the following year of '67. I knew that a few musicians had, indeed, experimented with the harpsichord in jazz, Arty Shaw among them. But no one in the world, it seemed, was at that time of '66 making a feature of it. And I knew a Tom Goff harpsichord would be the perfect vehicle for the concept.

Given that the Kirckman was eighteenth century, it had, at least, been restored by Tom and given pedals to facilitate the operation and nuances of the various stops. Tom still employed leather plectra for the lower manual, but had begun to use condor feathers to pluck the strings of the upper manual. He had previously used ravens' quills and had, indeed, found a useful source of supply from the keeper of ravens at The Tower of London. Moreover, at one stage, his great rival Robert Goble decided *he'd* like to try quills rather than leather or plastic for the upper manuals of his own harpsichords. So he trotted up to London from his workshop in Headington, Oxford, and innocently asked the keeper of ravens if he could have some feathers... 'Well, sir,' drawled the old keeper, 'there's a gentleman who comes here and drops me a fiver for some feathers. Perhaps, if you'd care to raise it, sir..?' The keeper's eyes glistened with hope of a shade more filthy lucre...

'May I enquire the name of this gentleman?'

'Mr Goff, sir.'

'Oh no,' hastened Robert Goble. 'Mr Goff is a friend of mine. I would not want to upset him.'

And that was that. Such gentlemanly behaviour is rarely seen these days, and has probably vanished for ever. Not that one could see a lack of confidence from either of these two harpsichord makers...

'Well, of course, we *do* know Tom Goff, Tony, and he is a fine harpsichord maker. But *ours* are more authentic, I would say.' The 'House of Goble' had spoken.

'I think I use better wood,' Tom would nonchalantly comment when I had arrived in my car – straight from Robert Goble's place in Headington, Oxford, to London and Tom's house in Pont Street, near Harrod's.

"If only those buggers would join forces, we might have the perfect harpsichord." (the sound of a Goff with the action of a Goble). The quote from a phenomenal harpsichord player of the era shall remain unattributable.

But before my 'two-year sentence' at Oxford and Burford was over, I had played my jazz numbers to Tom's sister, Moira Goff, one afternoon following lunch in Tom's house in London. The effect on Moira was such that I perceived my future to be that of a performer in the big wide world, and that I would extricate myself from the straight-jacket of supposed academia, snobbery and boredom in which I had found myself.

Tom's lively sister Moira was an intelligent, eccentric spinster who owned and drove an AC Cobra – the fastest production car in the world, I was told, before the Aston Martin DBS came along. 'I have a Bristol, as well,

Anthony. But that's a little slow. I prefer the Cobra: it's quick. When you put your foot down, it *goes*.' Wonderful stuff –from a lady of 70 plus. But her interests were widely spread. She had shares in EMI, she had style and the money to indulge her tastes which included dressing up young men who could not afford the luxuries of life. I played her my jazz numbers, and she exploded:

'Oh, how *exciting*.' She turned to her brother. 'Now, Tom. You *must* put on a concert for Anthony.'

'Yes, yes. I'm thinking about it.'

'Well, *put* it on,' she snapped. 'There's no time to waste. Get Ibbs & Tillett to handle it.' Ibbs & Tillett were perhaps the top classical agents at the time, situated in Wigmore Street, and they dealt with numerous classy gigs in London. So there it was: my introduction to the civilized side of music. In time, I'd have more than my fair share of grotty gigs in clubs and low dives. All part of life's rich pattern, of course.

CHAPTER 11

I look back on 1967 as the year in which I regained my freedom and sense of fun. For there is little a creative person dislikes more than the hand of ignorant authority laid upon him.

"Those who can, do. Those who can't, teach". Did not these famous words fall from the acerbic tongue of Henry Louis Mencken? Cruel, perhaps, for even a seed of truth can hurt. These days, alas, political correctness dictates a programmed mode of thinking for our society, fearful of exposing differences. I am informed by an old friend of mine that there will be a backlash to this state of affairs... I am still waiting. In the meantime, I keep myself occupied, scribbling and tapping out my thoughts for my own sanity's sake, if not yours, dear reader.

LONDON, LONDON... Every time I spotted the sign on my way back there from Oxford on Friday nights, I felt the exhilarating pang of homecoming, of release from the stifling conservatism, pettiness and small-mindedness which still surrounded me. Maybe it's because I'm a Londoner… Yes, you know. So did the author of the famous song. London may not be to everyone's taste, but if you think of it as a collection of villages rather than a vast, threatening metropolis, the picture changes. If one is lucky enough to live in a nice village, so much the better. We all know some pretty frightful villages, of course.

When it comes to competition, some of us shrivel up altogether. But if we have what it takes, we welcome it as a stimulating challenge rather than a daunting task to fear… Either you "eat life, or life eats you".

At last, September 1967 had arrived, and I stepped out on to the platform of The Purcell Room, on The South Bank, London, to face my audience… FULL HOUSE it said on the huge notice board in the lobby: ANTHONY SHARP – Harpsichord… Scarlatti, Bach and Sharp… Harpsichord by Thomas Goff.

Behind the stage, my new friend Terry Long occupied himself with his two large Philips tape recorders, stacked one upon the other. They were one thousand pounds each – a lot of money in those days – but Terry was an expert in the art of recording direct stereo. Fancy studios were not for him. He was one of the big shots of The Audio Fair in London, and his importation of Revox Tape Recorders into the UK, as far as *he* was concerned, did not stop there. Always the perfectionist, he would strip them down in his large workshop behind his house in Totteridge Lane, and reassemble and test each one till it was perfect.

His recording of that '67 recital (which I still have) would result in my first TV broadcast on CBC, Toronto, in April of 1968… 'Wow,' exclaimed the producer of the programme when he'd listened to the tape played to him by another friend, Peter Swann, by then the new Director of The Royal Ontario Museum. 'I didn't know anyone could play that fast – on a harpsichord.' Hardly commensurable with good musicianship, I hasten to suggest, but it got me the contract.

In The Purcell Room, I concentrated on the work in hand. After my scheduled pieces, I received four encores, and the audience roared their approval. Any artist should have been happy, but…

'I beg you, Tony,' implored Tom Goff after the recital, 'do not read the papers tomorrow. The concert was a great success. You should be pleased. The critics are silly, talentless people, and will only make you unhappy.'

I kept Tom's advice close to my chest till next morning. After all, Moira Goff had organized a wonderful dinner at her house in Brompton Square for that evening, which Tom, Jane Gray of Ibbs & Tillett, and close friends attended.

'*Dembrey*,' called Moira in her no-nonsense upper class accent, '*more* chicken for Anthony.' Moira had clearly given instructions to her butler, Dembrey, to feed the guest of honour. Why rush to look at those darned papers and read the cutting cynicism of those critics, pulling me to pieces? I was here, enjoying cacooned elegance tonight.

By next morning, I weakened, and could barely resist having a peep at The Telegraph which my aunt Bet had thrust in my hand… "What Mr Sharp did on the harpsichord last night, Hoagy Carmichael did much better on the piano". Serve me right. Tom Goff had warned me. My aunt Bet, who had attended the recital and with whom I would stay for a few months, had grown very angry on my behalf, and I managed to shrug it off with 'Oh well, perhaps they'll be a little kinder next time… when they realize I'm not a flash in the pan.'

Indeed, come the following Purcell Room recital in June '68, I would have the TV show in Toronto under my belt, plus a couple of BBC TV appearances. There's nothing like exposure to make people think again… The Telegraph was indeed somewhat kinder. And by the time of my Queen Elizabeth Hall concert in December of '68, the critics had positively settled down into a balanced view of Mr Sharp's musicianship. Besides, there were then other musicians on stage on whom they could pick, if they chose. It was good to see criticism evenly spread. Moreover, I had paid my guys well, taken them to dinner, and via a spin-off in the form of another Late Night Line Up on BBC 2, provided them, I trust, a useful little spotlight on 'the box'.

While still in my jobs at Oxford and Burford, I had written to Cleo Laine to ask her if she'd sing in the concert at The Queen Elizabeth Hall, down in London. I had booked the hall through Ibbs & Tillett a year in advance, and had already written five jazz carols with the great lady in mind. She replied with a lovely letter saying how much she thought the idea of classical music in the first half of the concert and jazz in the second to be a great idea. However, she explained that on that date in December '68, she would be involved in a big TV spectacular for ITV. She would love to sing at my concert, but unfortunately would have to say no. At least I would have time to find another singer. But please keep in touch, etc, etc.

Subsequently, I would meet Cleo Laine at her house in Wavendon, Berkshire, while broadcasting there with Marian Montgomery.

And it was Marian who finally agreed to do the concert in London. The line-up of the group was, I must say, somewhat unusual for that time.

Naturally, I did not employ drums for the classical: for one thing, I tended at that time to be a bit of a purist, and for another, the drummer happened to be Ronnie Stevenson – a big band drummer, used to belting it out and driving it along, but the wind section consisting of flute/recorder, oboe and bassoon all came into their own in the 'Sharp treatment' of the Telemann. I wish I had kept a copy of the programme, if only to recall the madness into which my musicians and I allowed ourselves to get involved. However, the concert was not a complete disaster, for we were asked to repeat the music of the second half for another Late Night Line Up on BBC Television.

Laurie Holloway, Marian's husband, and himself a very fine musician and band leader, sat and watched at home…

'You earned yourself a bit of money, there, Tony – on PRS alone.' Laurie was referring to The Performing Rights Society royalties that an organization such as the BBC is obliged by law to pay composers.

'Unfortunately, Laurie,' I replied sadly, 'I'm not yet a member.'

So the BBC got away with it.

By 1969 I was looking for work once more, anything to keep body and soul together. A friend pointed the way to a music shop in South

Woodford. They needed someone to demonstrate electronic organs, and ideally, to sell them. So I trotted along to meet the man and his wife. I can't remember *his* name, but June has stuck in my mind, if only for an amusing little episode which temporarily alleviated the drudgery of demonstrating Yamaha organs... I was sitting one day at one of these instruments, wishing it would turn itself magically into a Hammond M, when in walked a very nice-looking young lady, to make an enquiry about her new radio set. Without hesitation, June's dog, a large and enterprising Alsatian immediately put his nose firmly up her skirt, and kept it there.

'*Down*, Welly (short for Wellington),' said June, flushing up with embarrassment and apology. The young lady decided not to encourage the dog any further, and left the shop with business uncompleted.

No sooner had she gone than June's little grandson, ran into the shop and proceeded to play with his ball on the floor. June had gone into the back room, leaving Wellington to mooch about, searching for another naughty experiment. I was still seated at a Yamaha organ, in a somewhat better mood – after the recent event. What else would the dog get up to..? The young boy continued to play with his ball, completely unaware of Wellington's excitement behind him. The dog's penis was now erect and the animal had got himself into a comfortable position behind the boy. As he held on to the lad's shoulders with his paws, he begun pumping away. I cannot honestly recall the tune I was at that moment playing on the organ (could it have been 'Tea for Two'?), but I do remember calling June into the shop to point out the picture...

'Oh, *no. Down,* Welly,' she repeated, now clearly worried about her dog's enthusiasm and catholic interests. 'Tony,' she went on, '*Don't* let him do it.'... 'Not to the *boy.*'

I really don't imagine it had anything to do with these two amusements, but June and her husband got themselves into a bit of a financial jam, and were last seen doing a runner – by helicopter. I do hope they are both in good shape, this side of the grave, for I am grateful for that little job that would tide me over yet another bad patch of my own.

The year 1969 is also marked by two other events which stick in my mind: one, the reluctant sale of my Austin Healey 3000 Mk 3, albeit to a pleasant young man who had a fine business in Hay Street in The West End. Good luck to him. He used to dash around town in the car with his girl-friend, and one day allowed me to drive it once more. I wanted it back, but the sale had been made, and life is life. I needed the money.

The other event which I recall was the demo recording of a number of mine called 'Time to Wander'. It was written somewhat on the lines of 'A Whiter Shade of Pale': at any rate, it was very Bach-like, and almost everyone who heard it was moved by its haunting hook and melancholy. A guy called Mark Edwards decided to set up the demo in The Marquee Studios in Wardour Street. He produced a good sound, and screwed up the speed so that the singer's voice changed into an attractive lost boy timbre. The singer, who was also the lyric writer, was furious. I who had written the music, thought the result just the ticket. Anyway, Mark took the master tape to Pye Studios, and there another producer, Roger Taylor (with whom I became a close friend) decided he liked the number enough to 'pinch' it from Mark…

So, in the following year, 1970, the record was produced and put out by A&M Records to which company Roger Taylor had moved. When I turned up to the mixing session at Trident Studios I could hardly believe my ears: a 'Phil Spector' mishmash which obliterated the simplicity and unique feel of the original. My luck again?

CHAPTER 12

Looking back over the years, it would seem 1970 marked a further break from the straight-jacket of respectability and expected behaviour, and would lead me, if not exactly into the ways of wickedness, at least into a more 'colourful' life-style - in keeping with the enticing joys of the era: love and peace, sexual adventures, provocative clothes, great rock music, and even good weather (the summers of '75 and '76 spring to mind) – together with the feeling this was already too good to last.

In 1970 I changed flats, and moved to another part of Wanstead.

'Where are you living, now, Tony?' asked Dudley Moore innocently on the phone from the West End.

'Blakehall Road.'

'*Blackhall Road*?' he croaked cruelly in the Greater London accent most of us had come to know and relish through his TV shows with Peter Cooke.

I laughed and invited him over for a good old natter, drink and some music... He turned up in his jet-black Maserati, a lovely meaty machine with four-branch exhaust emitting a great symphonic sound, and a fridge in the back for the drinks.

He listened to the A&M version of 'Time to Wander', a number he loved, but agreed that Mark Edwards's version had the edge. Yet it was too late to change things... Then after listening to a tape of my Queen Elizabeth Hall concert, we sat and savoured a little of his own LP – 'Genuine Dud'. We sank into our seats, and a genuine tear trickled down Dudley's face as the music took him back to the time when Pete McGurk was alive and had not done the awful deed of suicide. 'He *was* a good bass player, wasn't he?' said Dudley wistfully. I agreed, but knew it was time to change the mood, so I invited him to play the Kirckman harpsichord that stood by the big bay window of my flat overlooking the dreaded *Blakehall Road*.

'Yes, Tony. It's a beautiful instrument. I'd love to buy it, but I've just had a tax bill I didn't know I would have to pay, a bill for Ten Thousand Pounds (a bit of money in 1970). And unfortunately my accountant is scrupulously honest.'

I think I replied with the obvious... 'Well, why don't you get one who's *not* so honest?' He grinned sympathetically, and went on to other matters.

It was just as well I did not sell him the harpsichord: I had offered it for thirteen hundred pounds. In April of that year, it raised Three Thousand Pounds at Sotherby's in London. I felt wicked for selling such a beautiful instrument in the first place, particularly as it was a gift from my friend Tom Goff. But he more than once suggested I do so, if I needed the money. Nevertheless, I knew instinctively he would have preferred I should keep it. My real consolation is that many years later a medium conveyed to me a message from beyond: 'He knows you needed the money, and that you would not have sold it otherwise. He is pleased it was useful to you at the time, and don't feel guilty.' I've long been a sucker for spiritualism.

Anyway, the sale of the Kirckman allowed me a temporary cushion and the opportunity to change direction and form a rock/classical group which I could take into the studio to record my new mad numbers... What crazy days they were: the landlord of my local was only too happy to see me spend money. I interviewed around a hundred musos out of the hundred and fifty who had responded to my ad in 'The Melody Maker'. After a chat and a 'blow' in my flat, I'd drive them down to the pub for refreshments. Needless to say, the Three Thousand Pounds (less 10% commission to Sotherby's) would quickly melt away if I did not take care, and I would have to put down a few numbers in the studio at my own expense.

This I duly did, once I had formed what I judged to be a good group. The result was a 'sort' of contract from Monty Babson of Morgan Studios. He seemed impressed enough to invite me into No.1 studio which would in time become my favourite in that set-up, there in Willesden Green, London. And it was there I would spend many hours, not only working on my music, hoping a record company would 'buy' it and the public at large would approve, but in the wonderful little bar that Monty had had built where the original studio had stood. I wouldn't say it was exactly my introduction to the pleasures of drinking – those I had discovered very early in life – it was just that the bar of Morgan Studios will for ever remain in my kinder thoughts as something never to be forgotten.

And at Morgan Studios I would come across so many faces - (don't take this literally) - Carly Simon, purring and oozing sex from the grand piano in Studio 1; Cat Stevens, young and charming - even before he changed religious direction and his name to Yusuf Islam, strumming away in Studio 2; Micky Most, hardly a mouse but a successful pop manager who would build himself a fancy house in Totteridge Lane, opposite my mate Terry Long.

Session musicians would abound, some cheerful, others somewhat morose. And, of course, the studio engineers: knowledgeable, helpful and very human. They had seen it all: groups come and go, the good and the bad, psychological cases, manic depressives, 'permanent' highs, happy, sad, wise, foolish, and an amazing number of thinking people with whom a good conversation was possible.

I had written some 'rock' numbers which featured the inevitable Tom Goff harpsichord, the loan for which Tom justly received a fee from Morgan. Moreover, he was never too proud or inflexible to mike up the instrument in the studio, or allow a wonderfully 'distorted' amplification effect through direct injection. The sounds that came out of the control room via that harpsichord were amazing, and well-matched the Hammond organ, Steinway Grand and Fender Rhodes available to me for most of the time.

On another occasion – a twelve hour session, in fact – we recorded my Rock Mass, adding four session singers (two from the famous King's Singers). My guys were fascinated to hear the lush sounds these few singers contributed to the music we had put down on tape. And how can I ever forget the fine musicianship of my band of merry men? First, the lead singer, Peter Ross – a tall, skinny, hairy and handsome young guy with a fabulous Joe Cocker-type voice (which years later would subtly change to a Stevie Wonder approach). Then there was Johnnie Franchi, half Italian, superb session musician, blowing happily and skilfully on his flute: he could make any sound I asked for, including a great Ian Anderson imitation (Jethro Tull). John played all the saxes, clarinet, bass clarinet... My God, what a player. Then there was Bob Taylor, lead guitar, with his 'Hendrix' sound and experiments, loving every minute; Andy Sneddon on bass guitar, steady as a rock with young Dave Neal on drums. Andy Sneddon had been involved in 'East of Eden', a group whose number 'Jig a Jig' shot into the Top Ten; and Dave Neal, a very pleasant lad and fine drummer, later joined Suzie Quattro's band. I myself was having a ball – writing, pulling it all together and playing those keyboard instruments that still gave me pleasure: Goff harpsichord, Steinway grand piano, Fender Rhodes, Hammond organ. Like Elton John, I have never been technical, but I surely wish I could have produced a sound like Keith Emerson (a rock idol of mine). He set up his Hammond organ like no one else, played like the devil, and then had time to throw knives at it and 'see to' a girl – all in the same number.

As to the business side and selling of my album... well, of course, I cocked it up, didn't I? Trying to be too clever, I tended to play record companies one off against another. I had my chances, and I blew them. My only hope – and it's a genuine sentiment – is that my guys have found it in their hearts to forgive stupid Tony Sharp. We all make mistakes; but mine were colossal.

The trouble is, I keep making them. Perhaps, now in my old age, I have calmed down a shade and found a reasonable compromise and contentment in living a simple life in the sun. Sex I have enjoyed in plenty; stress and disappointments I have endured; excess imbibing has brought me the bloody gout. Oh, bugger it: we are only human, and I have my memories.

CHAPTER 13

Yet much water would pass under the proverbial bridge before I could achieve a semblance of contentment. For as Andy Sneddon used to say to me, years after our experiments in Morgan Studios: 'You *love* living on the edge, don't you, Tony?'

Perhaps he's hit the nail on the head. Part of me yearns for my lost youth which I know will never return in this mortal life, whilst I pray a reluctant reach for maturity will not be exchanged for a complete disappearance of the joie de vivre. The achievement of a balance is a prize that eludes too many of us.

By 1972, I realized my attempt at a hit album was but a stab in the dark, and that reality would all too soon present itself. I phoned Marian Montgomery in my desperation to find work.

'Tony,' she said, 'where've you been? I need a piano player. Mine's run away.'

I laughed, and readily agreed to go over to see her.

'But you can't ask Tony to do gigs with you, Marian,' protested Laurie Holloway. He's a composer.'

'Oh, c'mon, Laurie. He's a genius. Grill him for a couple of days, and he'll be able to do it.'

So began my little run of gigs with the late Marian Montgomery. She was a brave lady, and on many an occasion she would introduce me to the audience and give me a spot... But as I've often said to friends over the years, it's a very dangerous move to give bloody Tony Sharp a spot of his own: he will surely up-stage you.

Indeed, one memorable evening in Hull at The Westfield Country Club (where they had been entertained by Lulu the previous week) Marian decided it was time to bring on the naughty Sharp... 'I have a young man, here (blimey, I was bloody old *then*) who composes his own music. You see him sitting at the piano, having done my stuff. Would you like to hear him doing *his* on the organ?'

'Yes, yes,' cried the crowd innocently. Well, Marian, bless her, handed over to me, and with a few more 'volts' through the electric organ, a nod and a wink to the bass and drums department to beef it up, I let fly. I was 'deputizing' for Keith Emerson, damn it. Who cared? We dug in, and the place went wild with excitement. Marian realized the danger in allowing it to continue and came rushing out of the green room, gave me a decided shove in the ribs, and turned to the crowd… 'He *loves* an audience, you know,' she drawled. The fate of the Sharp spots had been sealed for ever. I don't blame her. She'd not take any more risks in that department.

In the same year, Monty Babson renewed my contract with Morgan Studios. But I soon got into hot water when I foolishly took the advice of my music lawyer who could see how clever I had been, forming independent publishing companies…

It's a long, long boring story. Most professional musicians will tell you more than you'd want to know about the temptations, pitfalls and frustrations of the music business. Suffice to say, in *my* case, my 'cleverness' would blow back in my face (serve me right), and the contract with Monty would end. It would be another five years before he'd call me again – to have 'another go', by which time my style of composition, like me, had changed, and despite very happy times in the studio, nothing happened to the resulting music. Yet I parted company with Monty on good terms, and was able to continue the journey of life with a cleaner conscience.

I was still doing the occasional gig with Marian, particularly lunch-time TV appearances at Pebbermill Studios, Birmingham, but I decided to take a job as pianist/organist in a six-piece pop/dance band near Colchester: The Windmill, Marks Tey. And it was there I spotted Faith Brown, doing her thing on stage. At that time,

Faith was perhaps more a raunchy 'screamer' than the smooth TV comedienne she would become, and she certainly demanded a punchy backing group to support her powerful voice. Her drummer, whose name I have forgotten, approached me to consider 'going on the road' for a few gigs as Faith's keyboard player. After thinking it over, I did a week's turn at a club in Southport, Lancashire... Never will I forget one night when I suppose we were particularly loud, in response to her vocal vitality and provocative bosom, highlighted by the throbbing strobe lamps surrounding her. The drummer and bass player were going hammer and tongs, and I gave the Thomas organ full throttle. Suddenly, Faith's husband and manager, Len, came out on to the stage from the wings, shouting dementedly: 'What d'you think this is? The bloody Albert Hall?'

We all turned on block, the drummer leading the way: '*F… off.* '

Len turned puce with anger, and stomped back into the wings. But as soon as we'd come off stage, he sacked the bass guitarist, with the intention of taking his place the following night.

And on the next night, he realized what his wife's act was really all about. The club may not have been the Albert Hall, but Faith Brown needed *fire* from her band. This was not a quiet Quaker meeting in a sleepy English village. No more was said about the matter, from what I recall, and Len had calmed down.

In the summer of '73, I took off for a six week break in The States. I had been to New York after my TV stint in Toronto, and had flown back to London on a VC10. What a fine plane that was – with four Rolls Royce engines at the rear and a very strong fuselage and wings to keep the plane on course through the worst kind of weather. In my humble opinion, this plane was far superior to the Boeing 707 which, on the Toronto trip, seemed to bump and bounce around where it will. Or was it merely our captain's individual style? But in 1973 I took to the skies in a 747 Jumbo Jet – my first experience, and I must say, it impressed me greatly. Added to which, I sat and watched the fascinating film 'The Young Winston' during the trip. Winston, of course, had been our MP in Wanstead, and despite Mrs Wyebrow's lectures, enthusiasm and unbounded admiration for the great man when I was but seven years old and supposedly having a piano lesson, Churchill subsequently became my political idol. But then, perhaps Mrs Wyebrow *did* know what she was doing, after all.

The flight proved to be hugely enjoyable, and I landed in New York in a good mood. I checked in at The Piccadilly Hotel, 45th Street, and immediately felt at home. The hotel, sadly, is no longer there. The Marriot, though elegant in its massive way and doubtless fitting the bill as far as big business and shows are concerned, hardly matches the dusty intimacy of the old Piccadilly. For it was there, in the friendly bar near the Swedish food counter, that I met a few dusty old men who'd been in the theatre world for years and who had been on intimate terms with some of the great names of stage and screen. The late Bill Dean at that time managed not only the old Palace Theatre (where Judy Garland had made sensational appearances), but also the new Uris Theatre. He took me across to Sardi's in 44th St. for a pleasant drinking session with some of his more interesting friends. Bill Ross was there, co-producer of The Bilko Show, a wealthy man in his own right but burdened with an unwelcome problem of cancer. This did not seem to stop him chasing the young women and enjoying life as much as possible. It was he who gave me the contact with the vibrant Ann Croft who still lived in England. Ann had managed Benny Hill and Dave Allen and had married David Croft, writer of numerous successful sit-coms. Ann would subsequently treat me to so many elegant lunches in London that I stopped counting. I always sensed she would like to have managed me, but for my "death wish". For ever an intelligent, perceptive lady, she made a bull's eye remark to me one evening in my local wine bar, once she'd got to know me well: 'You know, Tony. You will never make it: you have that

Oxford degree and your little place in Spain. You are not *hungry* enough.'

I dumped my heavy bags in the locker at The Piccadilly, and took off for the West Coast, using my pre-paid tickets for internal flights. They were so cheap in those days, and uncomplicated by the serious need for security. It was just like jumping on a bus. Those days, alas, are gone for ever... I knew Laurie Holloway had been ensconced with Engelbert Humperdink as his MD in Las Vegas, and it was my intention to call on him before going on to Los Angeles. So I got off at Vegas, and searched for a phone at the airport. The heat wafting from the town into the airport building hit me with stifling intensity, and I had already made up my mind to go on to LA should Laurie not be there. I phoned his hotel and left a message. I'd missed him by a few hours: he'd left for another city for a one-off gig with Engelbert...

Up into the sky rose our plane to LA, and as soon as I'd landed and emerged into the sprawling city, I felt strangely at ease. I made for the Alexandria Hotel, down town, and booked in. There was a great bar, and a seated area with an upright piano – waiting to be brought to life. But I'd bide my time for the appropriate moment, and settle in. My room contained an outrageous king-size bed which would have accommodated a zoo, but I mustn't be greedy… I'll just make do with a siesta for now, and build up my strength. No sooner had I settled into the bed when my phone rang: it was Laurie Holloway. 'How's life? I'm sorry I missed you, but…'

So continued a musician's conversation about our peculiar life-style, fun, 'bitchiness', and behind-the-scenes carryings-on.

That evening I listened to the piano player downstairs in the bar, and decided that perhaps it would be politic to wait for a better moment before chancing my own arm on the 'precious' instrument. But I think I bought the guy a drink, and returned to the bar to await developments. I was in the middle of a conversation with the barman when I felt a healthy slap on my back together with the announcement: 'What the hell are *you* doing here?'

I turned to face a good friend of mine from Chigwell, in Essex, who was here on the West Coast with his girl-friend…

'Good God. It's *Pinky*. What a small world.' Pinky Ashton, as we called him, had an uncle – Sir Frederick Ashton, the celebrated choreographer, and though he never seemed to show the slightest interest in ballet himself, Pinky made up for it in an expansive largesse of good humour. He was always ready for a laugh, a good drink, and a helping hand to someone in need. 'Where can I get a really good steak at this hour?' I continued. Pinky pointed to a place a stone's throw from the hotel that had never closed for twenty-four years, day or night. After a celebratory drink with him, I left Pinky to enjoy his business with the girl, and made for the steak house... It was true: the place had been kept open for twenty-four years. Moreover, on the staff was a guy who had been washing-up for the last *fifteen*. Talk about a steady job. No worries, no real mental stress. Such excitement, poor bugger. But it takes all sorts to make a world.

I found the steak excellent, and cooked as I liked it. I was ready to take on the world, and glanced at my watch. What the hell? It was five in the morning, with no one to love.

Next day I came down to breakfast in the Hotel café. There had been a fire early in the morning in someone's bedroom. A man had been smoking in bed, and the place had caught alight. Pandemonium had broken out among the Orientals staying at the hotel, and they'd congregated in the foyer en bloc. But the manager remained calm and collected as he efficiently surveyed the work of the appropriate professionals. The fire was put out, the Orientals reassured, and God was back in His Heaven. I spotted the manager having a cup of coffee downstairs, and joined him at his behest. He knew I'd come from England, and wanted to hear about my work back there and my plans, if any, in

The States. As I began to give him a synopsis of my chequered career, he interjected with 'Tony, of course you may play our piano. Why didn't you ask the pianist last night?'

'Well, he seemed so content to be in charge...'

The manager laughed, understanding exactly what I meant.

At lunch-time, I sauntered into the bar, and went over to the piano. I cannot remember the make of the instrument, but it possessed a reasonable tone, so I continued awhile. Then after a couple of harmless numbers, a well-dressed guy called me over to his table to buy me a drink and have a chat. He introduced me to his friends, complimenting me on my individual style, and talked enthusiastically about his neighbour: it was Jimmy Webb.

'Oh, one of my favourite writers,' I concurred.

'I wanna be your lawyer if you come to live in The States,' he drawled with confidence... My God, such trust in an untried Englishman, I thought. Could this be an opportunity not to be missed, or just the lure of another lawyer's tongue, fanning my ego and leading me into disaster? I had been down that road the year before, when taking my lawyer's advice in London. To give that man his due, he did have the decency to say 'I hope I haven't f... ed your contract, Tony.' He had.

Anyway, I agreed to see this American guy again and go over to his house to meet his wife and family. What harm would there be in that? I might even get to see Jimmy Webb.

The same day, I decided to have a meal in the bar and another 'tinkle' on the piano. The barman made no objection, believing I would stick to a few romantic numbers. Oh, sod it. I felt like letting go. And I was off… with some Sharp 'classics' to get the blood racing. Another drink arrived on the piano, and a man with his girl-friend called me over to his table. 'You're very good,' he said with a grin. 'My name's Laine Montgomery. I need a pianist in my new revue in Santa Monica. Do you read music, and are you in the union?'

CHAPTER 14

Needless to say, I did not get to see Jimmy Webb. Sod's Law had conspired to place the man in London at the time. And the lawyer, well…

As for Laine Montgomery (no apparent relation of Marian), he remained unsure as to whether my Green Card could be obtained for me to take up his 'offer'. It was time for a change of scenery.

So I took off for San Francisco. What a lovely city, and all those happy people: of course, I'd arrived at the height of Flower Power, and it showed. Even the airport was laid-back and friendly, like nowhere else I'd known.

Pinky Ashton had invited me to stay with him and his friends, on the understanding I would not expect to be waited on hand and foot. Suited me. He even lent me the 'family' car, an old Chevrolet, to go out and do my own thing. I took the car over The Golden Gate Bridge to Sausalito where Marian had spent her honeymoon with Laurie Holloway so many moons before. After treating myself to another fine lunch of halibut and a leisurely stroll by the ocean, I stepped into a leather shop where I bought a beautifully-made belt of fine quality to wear with my blue jeans, and ponce about like the best of 'em.

Back in San Francisco, a quick glance over the bay to Alcatraz jolted me into the stark reality of other people's lives, less fortunate than mine. It's a good idea never to forget the simple adage: "There but for the grace of God, go I".

Many a laugh I would enjoy with my friend Pinky, but I sensed I may have unwittingly exacerbated a widening gap between him and his girlfriend. Even he had begun to tire of spending so much money on her, only for her to bugger off and return to England. Yet perhaps she genuinely felt a lack of true commitment on his part. For how could I forget her pertinent remark when we were on a visit to Disneyland, and her patience had run out? Pinky and I had stood, mouths open in wonderment at the sheer beauty and good looks of the young people marching along with the band in the closing parade…

'Come along, you two. Haven't you seen *enough*?'

And back in L.A., I had for a brief moment foolishly put my internal air tickets down on the check-out counter of a supermarket. The tickets disappeared in a jiffy, and the girl at the counter had "seen nothing". Luckily, I still had my Greyhound Bus Pass, safe in The Hotel Alexandria. So, but for an initial lift to Flagstaff, I travelled right across The States by Greyhound, stopping every three hours or so to stuff my stomach with junk food before returning to the bus for the onward journey. It was hardly my style; and those air tickets had gone. What would be the point of bemoaning the fact?

On arriving at Amarillo, I decided enough was enough and that I'd treat myself to a good night's sleep. There was a handy Holiday Inn nearby, so I checked in... At least the sleep did me good, and I felt fit enough to continue the journey towards New York...

The famous song says New York never sleeps: that's not the impression *I* had, for I arrived there at 5 a.m. with the place decidedly deserted. What goes on behind closed doors, of course, is another matter.

The contrast next morning – to see the city, teeming with traffic and people, blew my mind. Yet even these days, I still find myself returning every now and again to that special, mad place. It's like a shot in the arm, if you can stand the pace. Not that I'd care to live there: London would suit me better, if only I had the money to enjoy the city to the full.

But I could hardly leave New York without enjoying the fruits of The Newport Jazz Festival which happened to be taking place at that time. Dave Brubeck and two of his sons were doing their stuff in Central Park. So, too, was the late Dizzie Gillespie, strutting his world philosophy on the stage, and blowing uniquely and wondrously with those famous, inflated cheeks. A totally black chamber group impressed me hugely with their own jazz version of Bach's Passacaglia and Fugue in C minor which I remembered playing on the organ in straight, classical mode. I wish I could recall the names of the musicians, but I suppose I tended to be a bit of a dummy in those days. And still am.

I went to Shea Stadium to see and hear Stevie Wonder, but before he even appeared, the sound of the trains in the background and the noise of aeroplanes approaching their landings began to drive me mad, and I escaped the building to make a wild dash to the theatre where Count Basie and his orchestra were performing. I had missed the first half of the concert, but arrived just in time for a quick drink in the bar – where I appeared to be one of the very few whites present. Yet I felt completely at ease, soaking up the supremely happy atmosphere the black people generated. They smiled at me with love and unsolicited affection, for music would unite us.

Into the body of the theatre we trooped, and still I remained one of the few whites to be seen. The atmosphere was electric, and charged with emotion as Count Basie himself emerged and the band struck up with the first of a string of standards, and the crowd went wild with excitement yet would patiently anticipate the Count's famous, simple ending on the piano. The audience may have been sprinkled with few white faces, but I noticed a number of white musicians in Basie's new band. I was told the black guys had died off one by one, and a number of the survivors had decided to get in on the session circuit. The whites, in turn, had welcomed the chance to join the Basie Band before the old man himself kicked the bucket. They did the right thing.

High up over The Atlantic I listened to Stevie Wonder's latest number on my earphones – 'You are the sunshine of my life', – and I wanted the plane to turn round and go back to The States. I was returning home to England, to reality and to trouble. It would be a shock, if not to say shame, to suffer the embarrassment and consequences of 'repossession'. The previous year of '72 had proved pretty active for me, and I had acquired a small eighteenth century house in Colchester on the usual 'never never'; except, in *my* case, the mortgage had soon become unsustainable. After all, building societies are not exactly known for their sense of humour. Otherwise, the one with which I had been dealing might well have appreciated the idea of voyeurs gawping through the ground-floor window of the house, together with top-deck bus passengers getting a ring-side view of me having fun in bed upstairs. But the real crunch came with my stupidity in letting out the property to students whose even wilder activities alerted the authorities who wasted little time bringing matters to a head…

Having just returned from a pleasant trip to London, I attempted to turn the key of my front door, only to find the lock had been firmly and determinedly changed. Ah well, I still had all my limbs intact, though the brain had taken a decided bashing. What was I to do? I would go and talk to the Building Society to see if anything could be salvaged from the situation.

'This is a bad 'un, a bad 'un,' the man in the suit kept repeating, shaking his head with disbelief that I could have let things get so out of hand. 'Why didn't you tell us you were having difficulties? We might have allowed you to let the house as a business. But not to students, I fear.'

I smiled a knowing smile, and parted with a firm handshake, despite his wet one. I don't think he was too impressed.

But there it was. God knows how I survived, but I scraped by yet again. 'How does he do it?' people would ask. How indeed?

The return to London was inevitable. And I quickly became involved in the loose formation of an ill-assorted band of musicians with full pretensions of hitting the high spots. But I'd seen it all before, and so, thankfully, had two other members of the group. Suddenly I got a call from a muso about a gig in The Celebrity Club in Clifford Street, off new Bond Street...

So I went to see the boss – a 'big noise' in The Turkish Mafia, a pretty bright man and surprisingly amiable. I'd got a new gig, and roped in the group, now only too willing to get paid. Oh yes, talk is cheap. Money – even a little – does the real talking. There was a nice Knight piano on stage, and my group was booked to play for the show on a regular basis. Just as well we were all readers, since we had some strange acts to back. But mixed up with these were some genuinely funny comedians who helped to kick the evening along. One of these guys, however, was smartly sacked by the boss for making an unequivocal remark about the then British Prime Minister: 'How the hell can he run the country with a *cock* up his arse?' came over loud and clear. The audience, I believe, enjoyed the remark, but the boss had made up his mind. The comedian had to go.

The stage manager, who spoke like a Major General, chipped in with '*I'm* getting tired of the boss now, Tony. He gives a girl a fiver, and comes out of that little room, *buttoning* up his flies, and...' I tried to point out that the boss was in fact approaching our vicinity and within earshot. But the 'Major General' went on with increased confidence... 'What's wrong with a good *British* cock?' Pity, but he, too, had to go.

I myself moved on from club to club, strutting my stuff on whatever piano was made available to me. It would be years before I would have a Steinway on which I could express myself on a 'regular' basis and as a means of earning that precarious living. So, patience in abundance would be required of me in the meantime... 'The Twilight Rooms' springs to mind as a particularly grotty example of a nightclub where the girls appeared too tired and too bored to bother lifting their great legs in an especially grotesque stage act. 'The Gaslight', on the other hand, featured a bear, 'raping' a vulnerable girl, a spot which we were supposed to back with suitable music, without breaking into too much laughter. Another club featured a saxophone player in the band, a very nice man and a fine musician who was quietly 'biding his time'. I used to have wonderful philosophical discussions with him while we waited for customers to arrive. One night, *no one* had turned up, and I had been enjoying a particularly absorbing natter with him about reincarnation and the meaning of life while I sat at the piano, lightly brushing the tops of the keys with my fingers, to show willing. Suddenly, our drummer piped up with: 'I *think* it's time for our break now, Tony.' The sax player and I grinned at each other with priceless irony. Not a note had been played in the whole 'set' of around forty minutes, and we all quietly left the stage in our smart DJ's for a civilized drink at the bar. This was the famous 'Blue Angel'; a fair time, I fancy, past its prosperous days.

CHAPTER 15

I was driving my thirteenth car, given to me by a kind friend, and wearing a heavy green pullover and green corduroy jeans when I heard the news. The death of my mother, oddly, was not so much a surprise to me as that of my father. Yet, when it came, so many emotions rose to the surface, emotions with which I would have to deal in my own way and in my own time. High on the list loomed guilt, guilt that I had, like many a son, taken mother too much for granted, and in my case, given her too little money when I came to stay with her on the weekends during my unhappy period of penance as University Organist at Oxford; poignant guilt, too, for failing to raise just a smidgen of money so she could have her hair done, as she had requested when she'd phoned me from hospital – shortly before she died. How could I have been so callous and calculating? I felt in my bones she was near the end of earthly life and would not leave the hospital alive. Why did she need to have a hair-do? To look nice when she was laid out? Oh God, why *shouldn't* she? How could I be so cruel?

As I write this, I feel shame well up in me. Yet I know she has forgiven me. I am psychic and have seen ghosts, including hers – sending love and affection.

When the end came, I knew deep down I would make it up to her by my own love and ability to entertain others. She herself had a beautiful contralto voice, and her humour brought many a smile to an otherwise stoney face. Apparently, she is doing the same in the other world.

But my first task was to play the organ at the funeral. The service would be held at Christ Church, Wanstead, where in fact my parents had married; so too, both my sisters. I myself had risen through the ranks from choirboy to choir man and sub-organist, capable of 'carrying the can' at serious moments... But this was my own mother's 'do'. Could I do it without breaking down? What should I wear?

I possessed just one suit at the time: it was flashy white but fitted me well. Why shouldn't I wear it, rather than a borrowed, boring black affair, just to be like the others? The others were various members of the family and friends, most of whom, no doubt, thought me silly or disrespectful. But it was *my* mother lying there in that coffin behind me as I now sat at the organ, concentrating and eager to give of my best for her.

'Yes,' I could hear her saying. 'You look good, Tony. Nice and bright. Never mind the others. I'm with *you* .'

I wouldn't say it was the happiest gig of my life, but I did my best under the circumstances. And after the service, I took close relatives out to my local to cheer things up. My uncle Arthur remarked: 'You young people have the right idea.' … If you can call thirty-seven young. But I appreciated his sentiment.

A month later, a 'God-send' came along which took my mind off my bereavement: an Irish agent offered me a three-month gig in The Hotel, Formentor, north-side of Mallorca. He eulogized, quite rightly, over the hotel – its standing in the world and its stunning geographical position, together with its superb cuisine. I was hooked. But to achieve this prize, I would have to move fast. Could I form a suitable band in time?

I have to be honest and say that, by a long stretch, the result was hardly the best band for which I would be responsible, but if I didn't get my skates on, I'd lose the gig. I *needed* this break… Joe Vartan, an Armenian singer, living in London with his girlfriend agreed to join me as the front-line vocalist. He was perfect for the job: intelligent, suave, gifted and with a large repertoire. He could also speak five languages.

And what a diplomat he would prove to be; the bass guitarist was a young Jewish lad, very musical, a good player and easy to work with. The only real fly in the ointment, socially, turned out to be a fellow-Londoner: a good 'old' Cockney who could never quite bring himself to appreciate the situation – the beautiful hotel and its setting, the easy gig and general life-style, the fine cuisine and a rare opportunity to sample it. All he wanted was steak or fish and chips, pushing and shoving and the ways of London at its simplest and crudest. Shame. But, to give him credit, he wasn't the worst drummer I've known.

So despite a few embarrassing meetings with the hotel manager regarding the quality or otherwise of my group, we were not, after all, thrown out on our ears. It was a close-run thing, but we survived the three months, made a good holiday of it and bumped into a few faces. Even the late Oliver Reed approached me, *sober*, one night. He asked if one of his little girls might touch the keys of the Hammond organ which I played every night in the hotel club. He spoke in French, and I was grateful for Joe Vartan elegantly dealing with the situation in the language chosen by the great actor for his own personal and diplomatic reasons. This did not stop Joe giving us an analysis of the scene: Oliver Reed was on holiday with his French mistress and her two little girls. Who cared what the truth was? He had been extremely polite, and the little girl was made happy.

There was another actor in the hotel who bought us all a drink apiece, and whose voice I recognized, but not his face. Even when I got close in order to thank him for his kindness, I still couldn't quite place him, except for the fact he had been a regular actor in 'Hogan's Heroes', a popular American TV series.

The Hotel Formentor has always been a favoured haunt of the well-heeled actor or politician, for the management does its utmost to respect the privacy of its guests. The antics of musicians, however, are viewed with suspicion, and are hardly encouraged.

The three months at the hotel finally came to an end, and my band returned home, each member to do whatever he had to do. I myself felt a little at a loss, but remained glad of the experience, and eager to have more of the sun: such a pleasant ambience in which to make music. It would be the following year of '75 which would provide the opportunity. For the rest of '74, I would mooch around, picking up whatever gigs I could find and looking out for a place to put my head, if nothing else…

In this respect, the father-in-law of my old grammar school music master made a suggestion: he would approach The Rev. Eric Shipman and ask him if I could stay in Fairburn House – for a small consideration…

Fairburn House, Plaistow, was officially an establishment for trainee clergy, but had 'blossomed' out into a refuge for waifs and strays such as Tony Sharp and other oddities. It contained, offices apart, a fair number of bedrooms, large shower room with wash-basins, a commercial kitchen and a huge sitting/dining room where sat a beautifully kept Blüthner concert grand piano.

What could I say, but thank you very much, I'm happy to accept? Eric Shipman had remembered me as his Organist and Choirmaster at St. Andrew's for five years, and recalled those years with obvious pleasure and humour. He smiled, and offered me a bedroom, a regular first-class evening meal, and all facilities – for only seven pounds a week: cheap even for those days.

It was just as well I had a roof over my head and food in my stomach, since the gigs, such as they were, seemed to have dried up. Then suddenly, I had a call from Bob Grimm who had been a member of the American band 'The Four Seasons'. I had met Bob at Morgan Studios where he had been recording an album of his own material. Coming from the world of classical music, I myself had reached out to jazz, pop and rock in an attempt to bridge the gaps. He, in turn, was travelling in the opposite direction in *his* thirst for knowledge: he was a very serious American of

German stock. Yet we held each other in great respect, and would enjoy many deep conversations together. There is a surprisingly serious side even to yours truly, and I have to watch myself...

Anyway, Bob was now doing some arrangements for MPD – a breakaway group of The New Seekers. He roped me in with them for a few gigs as their keyboard player, and together they attempted to drag me out of what I hoped would be but my temporary doldrums. Civilized and pleasant as this work was, it was not sufficient, however, to sustain me for long, and it was fast approaching the point when I would have to call upon The Rev. Shipman's Christian aspirations and ask him to waive even my 'rent' of seven pounds per week... The downright cheek of it all. But Sharp got away with it once again. Then a friend found an advertisement in The Melody Maker for a Musical Director to a cabaret on The Angelina Lauro, a cruise ship sailing the Caribbean Islands.

But before this adventure began, I *did* pick up another night club gig at The New Embassy in Old Bond Street, W1. The club was run by a heavy Scotsman with the dirtiest Rolls Royce I'd ever seen, sitting outside in the street. That said, he seemed to take to me, and allowed me to find the players I wanted for the trio. After experimenting with a few bass players and drummers, I latched on to Craig Collinge, a very pleasant Australian drummer who told me he'd found an excellent bass guitarist who also sang. It was none other than Trevor Horn – now a millionaire and hugely successful pop writer and producer. Trevor took on the gig for a while, putting up with Craig on drums and fingers Sharp on piano.

But there were plenty of other dramas at that club to feed the senses and sharpen the proverbial wits. The Personal Assistant to the boss intrigued me for a time, not least for his apparent interest in The Caribbean and suggestion he should run a club for me on one of the islands. We had just been talking over the idea in a break, and I'd gone back on the piano to kick off the rest of the evening. Suddenly, news was brought to us that he had stabbed a man in the foyer, and killed him.

'Nice people, you mix with, Tony,' said one of my cynical friends later that night. But then, we musicians have to scratch a living, somehow. We find ourselves in all sorts of situations. We can rarely pick and choose.

During this time at The New Embassy, I would often miss out the first-class evening meal cooked for us and served at 7.30 sharp at Fairburn House. I hope I was not ungrateful for the offer, but the club gig did not begin till late, and I preferred the freedom to line my *own* stomach before tackling the onslaught of the evening. So I'd often cook myself a substantial meal in the big kitchen made available to us all. One evening I decided to have some calf's liver with spinach. The spinach was almost ready to serve, and I'd got the frying pan nice and hot, sizzling away with butter and herbal flavours when suddenly, without warning, an apparition, tall and white-robed rushed past my shoulder and disappeared right through the wall in front of the cooker. I turned on my heel, pan still in hand and gasped: 'Did you see that, Tony?'

Tony Franks, an intelligent young man, also staying at Fairburn House, croaked: 'Yes, I did. Not very nice. I wonder who *that* was?'

Ah well, life goes on. I cooked the liver and spinach: a delicious meal, and drove to The West End, to do the gig.

CHAPTER 16

What can I say about The Angelina Lauro? Sister ship to The Achille Lauro, later to be hijacked in The Mediterranean by Middle East terrorists who killed an old man in a wheel-chair, callously throwing his body and chair overboard, The Angelina itself endured an even more chequered career, before sinking in its berth at St. Thomas in the Caribbean as a result of a suspiciously convenient fire. Dutch-built like a sturdy galleon, and riding the waters like a lazy but powerful whale, the vessel was used as a hospital ship during The Second World War under its original name 'Oranje'. After the war, she returned to life as a passenger ship, sailing round the world. In 1964 she was sold to the Italian company Flotta Lauro Line, rebuilt and renamed Angelina Lauro.

At the time I clinched the job as MD to The Rex Grey Cabaret, The Angelina, now managed by Costa Lines, sailed from Port Everglades, Florida, calling at a number of The Virgin Islands and back to Port Everglades on weekly cruises. The passengers appeared to be mainly from Mid West America, intent upon enjoying themselves to the full. Most of them sported decidedly elephantine proportions and were seen to tuck into four large meals a day: full breakfast, lunch, dinner, and huge self-service cold supper – the tables for the latter feast taking up the length of an expansive corridor…

Who am I to talk, when it comes to food? In those days, I was lucky enough to be slim and fit as a fiddle, despite my love of good food. As musicians and entertainers, we were treated well, and ate the same fare as the passengers, though not necessarily in the same vast quantities. Nevertheless, for my part, it would get to the point when I would actually tire of the constant flow of lobster and caviar at our table, and pine (like my Cockney drummer of the Mallorca gig) for a bloody good steak and chips. Yet I could rarely fault the quality of the food provided us. After all, it was an Italian ship, and would hardly foul up the good name of its country's cuisine.

As for the shows we were obliged to perform each night, once the rigorous rehearsals were out of the way, they seemed to breeze along without too many hitches. Naturally, one could hardly forget a few incidents which made life a little lighter, and helped put matters in perspective. The cruise ships, of course, try to avoid the hurricane season altogether. However, there is certainly the odd occasion when a storm or at least strong winds can blow up and the ship will rock and roll with some persistence. One night when we were well into the show, my band driving the music and the girl dancers kicking up their legs with American-style gusto, I suddenly spotted a number of girls falter in their steps and the grand piano roll away from my hands, perhaps never to be retrieved. I had been given an unsolicited break, so why not have some fun from the situation? There was little point in chasing the piano all round the stage, although that would have been an act in itself. It would be wiser to wait patiently for its hopeful return. I simply smiled and waved to my drummer who felt obliged to continue playing to the bitter end. He was not feeling very well at the time… But as the ship righted itself, the piano returned to its original position, and I nonchalantly added a few chords to the proceedings to show willing. Cruelly I continued smiling at my drummer who told me, after the show, how much he had wanted to be sick. Yet I knew he would continue to play, despite his sudden attack of nausea. After all, he had come from a 'military' background. Nice lad, off stage.

Thank Heaven I had my own cabin. I would never have accepted the gig, otherwise. For when heated arguments break out and there is no way off the ship except to jump overboard, the private cabin remains a life-saver for one's sanity. Even then, I know I drank far too much (good malt whisky, of course) and even took up smoking again. I had not smoked since the age of fifteen, but somehow the pressures put upon me as MD on that ship began to invade my well-being, and I looked for a life-line. Silly, I know, but the temptation of two hundred Dunhill's for three dollars (two dollars to the pound at that time) was too great to resist. Luckily, I hardly inhaled the stuff, so for me it was easy to give up when the gig was over…

As for drugs, I have never been tempted. I tried cannabis once, as a 'gesture', but it meant nothing to me. Neither had I forgotten Andy Sneddon's words, back in '71: 'I've done it all, Tony. But it just makes me feel sick.' I decided to stick with alcohol, come rain, come shine. But even in those days, I knew I'd have to 'watch it' if I were to remain healthy. Would I heed my own advice?

At meal-times on The Angelina, our company had its own table. Not everyone took advantage of the regular meals, of course. Artists are notorious 'independents'. I'd miss quite a number of meals, myself. Besides, I soon caught on to a little trick of my own. It was decided we should have a day off in each week, enabling us to do our personal thing with some sense of leisure and freedom. Every Tuesday our ship docked in Old San Juan, Puerto Rico, for a few hours before sailing on to the pretty island of St. Thomas. But Tony Sharp had discovered he could fly over to

St.Thomas from San Juan for just seventeen dollars. So why shouldn't he have a dirty night *every* Tuesday, and catch the bloody ship the next day in St.Thomas?

The scheme worked beautifully till the end of the five months we were on that ship. But then I took on another gig – just for two weeks on a delightful little boat called The 'Italia'. It operated fortnightly cruises for older, richer passengers than those on The 'Angelina'. Again, I was given my own cabin, a good keyboard to work on, pleasant company and crew, and… Well, naughty Sharp played his trick once too often… 'Sleeping' in Old San Juan on the second of the Tuesday nights, the ship (like The Angelina) slipped anchor without my person on board, and made for St. Thomas. When on the Wednesday morning my plane hovered over its airport before landing, I looked down through my porthole to The 'Italia', resting in the bay. It was there, but somehow it *wasn't* there, as though it were merely a mirage, conjured up to taunt me. I got off the plane, passed through the landing procedures, and made for the club I'd discovered some weeks before. After downing a few satisfying drinks in the company of my new friends, I called for a cab…

The cab driver was very pleasant, and I had no feeling of foreboding until we were approaching the dock of St. Thomas.

'Which is your ship?' he asked in apparent innocence, yet looking out over the sea.

'The 'Italia',' I answered nervously, by now sensing trouble.

'*There's* your ship,' he said with unmistakable, cruel glee, pointing to a small dot on the horizon.

It took three days and all my week's wages to catch that ship, not, I hasten to add, without partaking of a little unscheduled sex along the way. Those were the days – carefree, unprotected, unsuspecting.

I caught up with The Italia in the port of Curacao, where I could still sense the presence of the Dutch masters of old on every wall and at every corner.

'Had a nice time, Tony?' called my friends from over the rail, as I jauntily approached the ship on my own two feet.

'Very nice, thank you,' I responded with mock embarrassment. Why should I be ashamed? Life is life, and they knew it, too. I would regard those days as an unplanned holiday, and return to England with another smile on my face.

But it was The Angelina that would spark off more than a few grey cells in my head, and awaken me to the realities of life. Sex is sex; murder is another matter.

On board were at least two murderers and not a few smugglers. As everyone knows, a ship at sea is its own government, and in our case, its own 'Vatican'. Most people have no idea of the way the world really works. If they *did,* either they wouldn't believe, or if they did believe it, they would go mad with anger or frustration in their inability to do anything about it.

But I have always been an observer. People fascinate me. There is nothing 'normal' about any of us. Each is a microcosm of competing energies, all trying to gain the upper hand. Rarely are we truly balanced and mature. And when we are, we can be as boring as… No, hell isn't, is it?

Anyway, at our table, I would sit next to an American guy whose girlfriend was one of the dancers in our company. He exuded a quiet calm about his person, and would puff away on his cigar while he examined you. I could feel this, yet we intrigued each other to the point where our mutual discussions developed into two conversations, held at the same time. Under this cover, we could probe each other while keeping the rest of the table in blissful ignorance. It was a game, but not unpleasant. In fact, over a quiet drink together in one of the bars on the ship, this man (I'll call him Mark) bought me my favourite cocktail, expertly mixed, shaken and poured by the barman, and continued to pursue his line.

'I see you have a head on you, Tony. Would you like a business of your own?'

I looked at him with a cautious smile and asked: 'What kind of a business have you in mind?'

'Say a piano bar on one of the islands?'

'Which one?' I was really listening now.

'How about where we're heading?'

'St. Thomas? 'Um, very nice. Let me think about it, Mark.'

'Okay. Take ya time. I'll put up the money; you run it the way you want, and we'll split the profits. Like another of those?' The chichi the barman mixed had tasted wonderful: vodka base, crushed ice and grenadine.

On the island, Mark introduced me to a friend of his who ran a large spread on the beach called The 'P' Club. I shook hands with him, and made for the bar. As I waited for Mark to return, I studied his friend, standing alone and 'distant' on the beach, looking into nowhere. And then it spoke to me, my inner voice saying: 'Beware. This man 'smells'. Check out his connections.'

On the way back to the ship, Mark and his girlfriend strode out with apparent ease and happiness. He had just bought her a beautiful diamond which she was eager to show off.

'Very nice indeed', I responded genuinely. ''Course,' I continued, now looking directly at Mark as he walked along, pulling contentedly on his cigar, 'you're not a *free* man, are you?'

He took the cigar from his mouth, and looked me in the eye with surprise and suspicion. 'What d'ya mean, *free*, Tony? I live like a King. I couldn't live like you in England, scratching around for gigs. So, what d'ya mean *free*?'

'*Really* free,' I answered, and immediately regretted both the remark and the emphasis I'd put on the word *'really'* together with its implication. Mark shot me a serious side-long glance, and I knew I'd gone too far. Luckily, his girlfriend distracted him with something she'd seen: 'Oh, look over there, Mark' which helped to take the heat out of the moment.

The next day, a proper chat helped to clear the air. Mark had been busy counting the money from the slot machines. All the customers had departed and gone to their cabins or favourite bars. I had drifted into the area with perfect timing, it seemed. We were alone and able to speak our minds without restraint or fear.

'Tony, you were saying something to me yesterday. What d'you mean by *really* free?'

'Well, Mark, if we were to go into business together, I'd want to know everything about you. You may ask me anything about myself, too, and I'd tell you.' He looked up to me with close interest, but held his tongue as I went on: 'I might have gone to a fancy old university, but I'm still a Londoner, and straightforward. I hope you appreciate that.'

'I do, very much. And I like you. But I want your word that what I'm about to tell you will remain strictly between you and me – until we are off this ship. Have I your word?

'You have.'

'Good. Well, I'm a hit man.' He stopped and waited for my reaction. I didn't shake or shiver but merely said:

'Everyone has to make a living. It would not be my choice, but that's life.'

Mark visibly relaxed at my words and calm demeanour. He could sense I'd 'been around' and had 'seen things'. Then as I was about to change the subject he offered to tell me more. 'Of course, there's another murderer on this ship: one of the offi…'

'Okay, Mark. Don't tell me any more.' I already had a shrewd idea of his identity.

A week went by, and Mark's girlfriend approached me with a curious announcement -

'You know, Tony, there's something funny about Mark. I can't put my finger on it.'

'Well, you're engaged to him, aren't you? Chat to him. *I* find him very interesting, well read, intelligent and easy company. I don't know what you're talking about.' A white lie, perhaps. But I had given my word to the man: an Englishman's word *used* to be his bond. Mark had requested I should keep silent until our gig was over and we were off the ship. In fact, I kept quiet about it for *years*, and I'm glad I did.

Just before we all disembarked from The Angelina, Mark and I wished each other all the best. He knew I did not wish to go ahead with a business arrangement, and he had quietly accepted my unspoken decision. Maybe his girlfriend knew more about him than she had let on, and I had passed 'the test'. For he could not resist offering me his services should I ever require them...

'Don't worry, Tony. If you need anyone out o' the way, don't hesitate. It's twenty thousand dollars.'

That was in 1976. Twenty-five years later, I met a man in my bar in Spain who offered to kill my neighbour for five 'grand' (English money). 'That's very reasonable,' I told him, unfazed, and carried on pouring drinks to get him drunk. If I'd really been serious in giving the man the go-ahead (for I had the money at the time), I knew I'd be suspect No.1 for the murder. Besides, unlike the professional gunman I'd met who invariably hit the target, *this* man would probably have missed.

CHAPTER 17

1976 just has to be about the best English summer in my living memory. From April till the end of October, the glorious weather brightened our lives and predictably caused panic and hose-pipe bans across the country.

The Caribbean gigs had ended in April, and I returned to the old country with a smidgen of money, a healthy colour, lots of experience under the belt, and nowhere to live.

'You can stay here till you find a flat,' offered an understanding friend in Wanstead, the place of my birth, childhood, and 'adult', reckless fun. Anxious not to overstay my welcome, I feverishly scanned the papers for that elusive flat. Lady Luck had decided not to desert me altogether, for I spotted an ad for a small pied-à-terre in Hyde Park Square, W2 at what appeared to be a very reasonable rent.

And what an address, even if it turned out to be a broom-cupboard. It was not far off the mark, yet self-contained, and consisted of a tiny room with 'single' bed, wardrobe, drawers and simple table, bathroom and cooking area. Thank Heaven I do not suffer from claustrophobia, otherwise I'd never have survived there for twenty odd years. Besides, the flat was to become the setting for abundant histrionics and not a little sex: all part of life's rich pattern. And how convenient for my work. I could walk to many of the gigs, use the buses or trains, and, good fortune willing, the occasional taxi.

So I now had no car, for the previous year another piano player had purchased my old MGB. To my mind, that machine hardly compared with the Austin Healey 3000. But for a mere one hundred and fifty pounds, how could I complain? And yet it had finally dawned on me that a car in London can be more of a liability than a convenience. After all, in 1975 I had been playing in West End night clubs whilst actually living in East London. What was the point in working my 'proverbials' off till the small hours, only to drive back to East London, and then have to return next night to the West End, and repeat the process ad nauseam? 'Wake up, Tony,' said the small voice. 'Find a flat in West London, and get rid of the car.' Whenever I listen to that inner voice, I land on my feet. When I ignore it, I fall flat on my face. It's all very simple.

So now there was no car and as yet no work. But I had clinched the tiny pad. The caretaker lady, Olive Gaca, would in time become one of my best friends. Ever understanding, she possessed a good sense of humour, a fondness for a tipple of whisky or brandy, and a love of cats. Her psychic powers, too, would draw us to each other, and we indulged in many a perceptive discussion in her large flat in the basement. Years later, I would name one of my cats Herbie, after Olive's extraordinarily 'knowing' little cat who, she remained convinced, had "been here before". At least two others are buried in the square gardens: Arnold, the beautiful black beauty who, sadly, suffered traumatization at the hands of some of the men, working on a house in the square; the other, Eister, who reminded me of Miss Piggy in The Muppets with similar hair and those 'distinctive' ears. What a funny little cat. In fact, I remember cooking a couple of steaks on Olive's cooker in the basement. Suddenly, I turned round to see why Eister had been making such an unhappy, whining noise, more like a human than the acceptable, characteristic meow of a cat...

'What's the matter, Eister?' I asked her, as 'human to human'.

'Don't know,' she snapped without hesitation. I could hardly believe my ears.

'Did you hear that?' I exclaimed to Olive, with happy, incredulous surprise.

'Yes, I did, Tony. What an extraordinary girl she is.'

If that flat of mine could talk, what a story to fill a book. But would it ever be published? Naughty is hardly the word. Suffice to say, if I were to die now – an event which is, as for us all, inevitable one day – I could say to The Boss, with my hand on my 'heavenly heart': 'Well, sir, some people would want to curse you for such a rough time, but… may I put it this way… thanks a million, mate.'

But it wasn't all sex. Serious, all-pervading discussions and arguments were held in that bolt-hole. The late Bernard Bresslaw visited me there to discuss a book I'd written which on first reading had disturbed him. It was called 'The Guv'nor', and was my first fantasy novel.

'I can't take that Hitler bit,' he said with conviction and some vexation. But he had missed the point of 'that Hitler bit' in the book. Of course, Bernard was pure Jewish and a lovely gentle giant of a man in my estimation. I, too, have some Jewish blood of which I am far from ashamed. But there must surely be a balance in life. I was determined to release Bernard from his cage of prejudice and preconceived, if understandable judgements…

As he sank into my leather sofa, filling it, it seemed, with his huge frame, he burst out with honest humour: 'Well, Tony, I've heard of pieds-à-terre. But this is *ridiculous* .'

I laughed, and moved to open some bottles. 'Don't worry, Bernard. We'll take these and the chicken into the square. You'll be able to stretch out there.' He smiled as we made for the square with enough food and drink for a decent meal. He had already begun to brighten up, and we were soon tucking into a freshly roasted chicken from the local delicatessen, a nice salad and a couple of bottles of Sancere which I'd extracted from my fridge. He felt much better after that, as did I. The meal had done the trick, and he seemed ready to discuss the book anew.

He listened with commendable concentration to my explanation of The Guv'nor's purpose, and he appeared to accept my plea that I was not at all anti-Semitic and that I loathed the Nazi regime and its ethos. However, and this is the point – only *God* can adequately judge mankind. 'But for the grace…' and all that, I went on. 'Take that man, that woman, that boy and girl walking round this square: each could, in the right or 'wrong' circumstances become a Hitler. Good and evil are really the same source: energy. We have a choice to turn left or right. And now, The Guv'nor is going to turn Hitler's energy to good, and the Prince of Darkness becomes the Angel of Light. Get the idea?'

'I see what you mean, Tony.'

Bernard subsequently became a champion of my book, and did his best to gather together a coterie of interested actors and actresses for a film version. Unfortunately for me, Bernard died, and with that sad event, so did the dream of a film. My luck once more? Or is God not so silly, after all?

Even Dudley Moore visited me in that cramped little pad with his third wife, Brogan Laine. This was later, in 1991, a year before I escaped to go and live in Spain on a permanent basis. And I remember my aunt Bet saying 'Oh, Tony, you *can't* ask him to come and see you there.'

'Why not?' I responded. 'He's used to better things, I know. But he's seen even worse, in his time. Besides, he's coming to see *me*, not the bloody flat.'

'Oh, Gawd,' she groaned predictably. Bet could never quite bring herself to accept the sheer perversity of her nephew, nor, it appeared at the time, the possibility that Dudley and I might share a similar twisted sense of humour. After all, like me, he had come from East London, and he'd seen *Blake Hall Road*. He might well have believed my new flat in such a prestigious area of W2 would be an improvement, but…

The bell rang, and I answered the entrance phone.

'Dudley.'

I pressed the button to let them in, and trotted down the short run of stairs to greet them. Tall, sexy Brogan stood back to allow Dudley and me to have our little Cockney cuddle of affection. And then a hug for Brogan while Dudley climbed the stairs and stood stock still at the top - to witness the shabbiness and constriction of my tiny pad for himself. But he graciously said nothing.

After a few drinks and a good old natter and laugh, we made for the restaurant, and tucked into calf's liver, spinach and some good wine.

'Now, let us pay for this, Tony,' he said when we'd finished.

'No, Dudley. You always paid when we ate out in the 70s and 80s. I want to do this one.' Which I did. I had no idea it would be the last time I'd see him, bless his soul.

CHAPTER 18

The little piece of money, accrued from the Caribbean, was fast disappearing. Would I be able to hold on to my cubby-hole in Hyde Park Square? The address might fool a few impressionable oddities, but hardly my relations or close friends who knew it for what it was.

Why should I worry? All I needed was a job. A job? Have you gone mad, Sharp? Musicians don't have jobs. Panic…

I phoned a drummer friend of the name George Cummerford (naughtily called George *Cumbersome* by Pete Dennis, a superb bass guitarist at the time). George had a gig for me: keyboard player in a band working in The Bizzarro, an Italian restaurant in Paddington.

So I joined the group for a residency there, enjoying the good food and wine, the ambience and not least the convenience of a very short walk to and from my flat. The music covered the whole range of styles, and the band was led by Darryl Green, a black all-rounder who fronted the group as lead singer and guitarist. Darryl possessed a lovely voice, full of pathos and nuance, not unlike that of Lionel Ritchie.

Most of the guys could not be bothered to eat the delicious food provided by the management before kick-off. So 'gourmet' Sharp would get stuck in on his own – with a good bottle of Italian red to hand.

'A *whole* bottle to yourself?' Luigi, the harder of the two bosses, loomed over my table with wonder that I could manage it without falling over or becoming incapable of doing my job. 'Of course, Luigi. Don't worry about *me*. I'll play well, after this.'

Luigi remained unconvinced, but let me be.

The softer of the bosses, Antonio, even lent his Maserati Indy to Darryl, so that he, Darryl, could take out his girlfriend and impress her over the Christmas period. How many Italians would do such a thing for a musician? But Antonio was an 'old softy' and we all loved him for it. Both he and Luigi possessed a Maserati Indy, and when these cars were parked one behind the other by the kerb outside their restaurant, they gave the impression of two sleek, eager seals, preparing to breed new baby Maseratis.

Bizzarro was the restaurant to which I chose so often to take my kind bank manager, Tom Lee. At least three times a year, he would treat *me*, 'on the bank'; the other three occasions I'd treat *him* – on my overdraft: same bank. For years the scheme worked beautifully, since Tom was of the old school of bank managers: a thorough gentleman. Besides, he had grown tired of the constant flow of shop-keepers, wine-bar owners, estate agents and the like. To have a mad musician as your friend and client, albeit hopelessly impecunious, was a relief from reality and, to him, a breath of fresh air.

'I'm not worried about you, Tony,' he would say with a smile over our kidneys and dressed salad, whilst I would sit with contentment and gratitude for my luck in finding such a banker as a true friend. He never let me down, and I hope I never let him down. I'd love to feel he has not regretted taking me on, despite such dubious prospects and entrenched hand to mouth existence on my part.

Tom was indeed a lovely, human man. And over one of our memorable lunches, I asked him what he intended doing for himself…

'I think I'll take early retirement, Tony. I make millions for my bank, and *still* they are not satisfied.'

'Usual greed,' I concurred. But he went on…

'They say to me: "Why d'you take people out to lunch? They're just a number."'

'Ah, there'll come a time, Tom,' I said, 'when customers, even poor ones like me, will demand service, and *get* it.'

'I agree with you, Tony. But *they* don't see it.'

And how can I forget our pre-lunch drinks in my tiny flat to get us in the mood for good food? Tom was very fond of vintage port, and so was I. Once again, I had seen most of the cartoons of port-lovers, and brushed aside the idea of gout as totally inappropriate. There'd be time enough for such an absurdity.

Round about this time, I was asked to write the music to a stage version of Reynard the Fox, and bring it out of hiding to be a musical for the general public. Someone, completely unknown to me, had written what I felt to be a rather long and turgid script. Yet my friend Jill Racy, who lived in a very pleasant area of Clifton, Bristol, appeared keen to write the lyrics, and roped me into the project... Oh, it's a long, long story, involving on and off-stage drama of the most intense, bitter kind.

Suffice to say, the 'musical' was staged in the spring of '77 at Watford Palace Theatre. And it was there, in the show, that I met Bernard Bresslaw, Murray Melvin, Elizabeth Romilly and a group of other talented actors who cheered me up considerably. Besides, I got myself a 'job' as MD to the show, directing from my Fender Rhodes piano and Hammond organ which I'd used in The Bizzarro restaurant in Paddington.

From my days at Morgan Studios, I had never forgotten the musicianship and brilliance of Johnnie Franchi and how delightful it always was to work with him. So I twisted the arm of the manageress at Watford to give Johnnie a little more money than he had been getting in the West End to come and play flute and saxes for us. I also managed to book Glen Le Fleur on drums (a session drummer with great feel and style) and Geoff Hull who had played bass guitar on The Angelina Lauro.

To cut a long story short, the show ran for the scheduled three and a half weeks and, quite properly, in hindsight, was *not* transferred to The West End, despite its potential…

'It makes me *mad*, Tony… Your music is so strong, and wasted on that *f…ing* script.' Bernard Bresslaw let fly a torrent of words as well as urine, as we stood together, having a slash in the toilet during rehearsals. But what could I do, but bite the bullet, be grateful for the gig, and look for the next project?

After the Watford run, I received a call from Morgan Studios… 'Are you interested in doing some more of your stuff over here?'

Well, of course I was interested. So, with new material, I went into the studio with some of my chosen guys. This time, I succeeded in procuring them session fees, which helped things go with a swing. Interestingly, The Swingle Singers were also available 'for hire', and I picked out a few of them to record a silly but fun choral/instrumental piece of mine called 'Someone's playing the fool up there', a fugal number which I figured would be just 'up their street'. They had become a popular close-harmony group, and like The King's Singers, highly professional.

One of my favourite tracks on those Morgan sessions, however, turned out to be a song called 'Easy for me to get by', a 'catchy', jazzy number to which I also penned the cynical lyrics. But who cares? You, dear reader, I'm sure, have never heard the song, and probably never will…

Monty Babson listened to the tracks I'd done in his studio with interest and surprise…

'Lovely stuff, Tony. But you've changed your style. What's happened?'

Six years is a long time for me. My style of writing had indeed changed, together with other aspects of my life and outlook. An artist experiments and pushes the boundaries in pursuit of an individual path. The businessman's world is by nature on a narrower track, and one can count the visionary on one hand.

But I still had to feed myself. And then, a little gig in Welling, South London, turned up. Yet I had been given to understand that *humour* ran as far as Catford, and no further. Lucky for me, my informant would be proved wrong. The Greek restaurant owner not only displayed a fine sense of fun, but he even lent me his Escort van in order to travel between Hyde Park Square and his restaurant on the other side of the world. It was a good gig, and there I met a young singer by the name of Janet Stevens whom I got to know well and with whom I'd subsequently work in The Middle East for several months.

It's strange how life works out. As for life itself, I shall never cease to wonder... Take care what you say, Sharp. Yet the gig in Sharjah in The United Arab Emirates provided me with a pretty good insight into a strange world of intrigue, opulence and parallel poverty, face-saving humanity and idiocy, and a profusion of luxuriant, happy rats.

For three months, we, the band, performed in the restaurant of the motel, run by Lebanese businessmen. The drummer of the band was Lebanese himself and was officially the boss, since he got us the contract. But like life itself, there were a number of eruptions between members of the group, leading to a break-up after three months...

Various factions emerged, hoping to catch the ear of the management. As this childish behaviour began to get out of hand, I went to the management and offered them the services of Janet and myself.

'Just what we want, Tony. We like you and Janet. We will give you both a new three month contract. Happy?'

When tempers had finally subsided and the band returned to England, no doubt in a bit of a huff, Janet and I proceeded to do our job without fuss. But it was not to be without its own particular dramas and amusements...

One fine night, Janet looked especially elegant, with her long, flowing hair draped over an attractive white silk dress as she sang her love through a plaintive Carpenter's number. I had adjusted my Fender Rhodes to what I judged to be a perfect, smooth accompaniment to her voice; and it was all going well. Even a few tears of appreciation could be seen to fall down the faces of normally stiff customers, sitting at their tables over coffees and liqueurs. Suddenly, a huge rat who had been patiently waiting under a nearby table for his chance to get at the remaining food left by customers just gone, got up on a high-back chair and lifted his head towards Janet, cocking his intelligent ear to the song. What an honour, if she would only see it that way.

I kept playing the Fender and turned to point out the picture: 'Oh, look at that, Janet. Isn't he funny?'

Frozen in terror, Janet had tried to scream, but nothing would come out. In her panic, she dropped the microphone which fell to the floor, and dementedly she ran off the stage, mouth open in total horror. She went up to our apartment, whence she would not return. The musical evening had definitely been written off. The rest of us, I fear, had a good laugh at her expense.

On a subsequent evening, when the rat episode had passed but not entirely been forgotten, Janet had dolled herself up once more and would no doubt attract a few customers to her charms, if only at a distance. Yet, there is always the odd guy, even in a humble motel, who might fancy his chance of a night of lust, albeit at a price. Not that Janet was such a girl. She was not. But men are men, and I never forget being called across to the table of a very presentable gentleman who asked me to join him over a drink or two. What had I to lose? A drink is a drink in my book, and I prided myself on being able not only to look after 'No.1', but someone else whom I respected and of whom I was fond.

The man turned out to be a very bright Armenian in the oil business, and we chatted away like two close pals of old until it suddenly dawned on me that he was not here just to be friendly. His constant reference to Janet and how nice she looked together with a continual increase in the monetary offer *should* have alerted me to the real situation at hand. It was a novel experience to be taken for Janet's pimp, albeit able to play a few chords on an electric piano for good measure… The price rose even further, and I was becoming quite pleased with myself in my new 'role'. But the man quietly assured me that 23,000 Dirham was quite a lot of money, and that he would have to stop at that...

'No, she won't,' I had kept saying.'
'All right. Let's have another drink, Tony.'
So very civilized, I thought.

The next morning, Janet had an announcement to make. 'I worked it out, last night, Tony. It was exactly *three thousand pounds*, Sterling.'

'Oh Janet,' I said, feeling very guilty and more than a heel, 'I hope I haven't f...ed your gig.'

Much to my relief and joy, she laughed out loud. 'No,' she went on, 'I wouldn't have done it, even for *that*.' What a girl, and what a sense of humour.

Before our three month contract was up, we were given the opportunity to go straight to Bangkok if we chose to take on yet another three-month stint - and with *double* the money. Janet and I discussed it, of course, and perhaps if the management had allowed us even a couple of days break before the new gig, I might have agreed to go. Janet herself was not bothered. 'It's up to you, Tony. If you want to do it, I'll go with you. But if you prefer to return to England, I'm easy.' Janet was one of those odd young women, not in the least mercenary. How refreshing.

CHAPTER 19

So to England we returned. Janet went her way; I went mine. Perhaps it was just as well I did not take that gig in Bangkok, since I might have missed the chance to clinch the residency in a very lively pub in Hoxton Street, London, a gig which lasted *eleven* years. This kind of job is very rare indeed, and but for its stability and someone who made sure I always got paid, I doubt my bank manager, Tom Lee, would have lent me the money to buy the little house in Spain. My niece's husband, a respected chartered surveyor was heard to remark: 'Tony won't get that money to buy a house. He's got no security.'

'He will. You watch him,' replied my confident, gutsy niece.

She was right. And the irony was that Tom Lee knew I was being paid by stable, well-respected villains. 'I think you have a steady job, there, Tony,' he said, much to my delight. 'I'll lend you the money.' Who am I to complain? But all this was a few years away.

I had not been back in London long, when my phone rang optimistically: it was a call from a bass player who needed a pianist urgently for a few gigs at The Bacchus, a rough and ready pub, he said, but with governors who were dead keen on music.

I shot over there, and it was what we Londoners call a shit and saw-dust pub, but in this case, without the shit or the saw-dust, if you get the picture. But I am a person for ever sensitive to atmosphere, and I liked what I saw: a guv'nor with a great 'Sinatra' voice, and his father, the 'naughty' man with the drive, personality and determination to succeed. They seemed to like me, too, perhaps because I played their resident piano with such enthusiasm and sported not only a fine, healthy colour, but a summery tee-shirt which showed off my newly-flexed muscles to advantage. Ah, those were the days. What an image – long gone, I fear.

The bass player said he had another job he had to do, and the guv'nor asked if I'd like to take over. So began the longest-running gig of my life.

Meanwhile, amazingly, I had still not quite exhausted the bit of money I'd made in Sharjah, But it could not be too long before it, too, would shrivel to nothing. It was just as well I had The Bacchus gig.

But in '79 I was approached by an Italian businessman, Peter Tolleni, to become the first piano player of a new bar he was about to open in Piccadilly. He told me the room, for him, had always been a lucky one: and here, I read plenty of sexy girls and plenty of money. But The West End was changing. Gay clubs were springing up all over town, and AIDS had not yet hit the UK. Peter had long been an astute businessman. He remained a happy heterosexual, but he could see the days of tinsel-girls, hostesses, outrageously expensive drinks and pricey sex already numbered. He was about to turn his 'Latin Quarter' in Wardour Street into a huge gay disco, and his 'lucky' room, 'La Belle de Nuit' into a gay piano bar in Rupert Street. It was to be re-named 14 Club. Would I play?

Peter had done a deal with two eager guys whose presence and business acumen would make sure the project was a success. The piano – an Ibach boudoir grand, and quite a nice machine – was already installed. All I had to do was turn up and play. ''You sure?'

So began a run of mixed gigs. Whilst I played at 14 Club during the week, The Bacchus, for me, developed as a weekend stint, and sometimes I'd 'double-up', jumping into a cab outside the pub and wooshing off to do the West End number. Those were the days, when I had energy and when I took joy in doing one gig after the other: the fingers were warm and in trim, the body willing, and the adrenalin was pumping... Now, now, you lot.

It was in the 14 Club that I met Henri van der Zee, a charming and successful journalist from Holland whose book 'William and Mary', co-written with his English wife Barbara, has become a classic in the annals of historical biographies.

Henri spoke with passion and love about his house in Spain:

'Oh, but if you need a holiday soon, Tony, use *my* house. We live in a little town by the sea, with the mountains around us, and...' He continued to eulogize.

And it was Maria, the street's house-cleaner, fixer, confidante, friend and fine-looking woman who took a shine to me during my stay in Henri's house. She had made up her mind I'd have first option to buy my little place when the time came.

But I had been warned. Only a few years before I met Henri, I stood at the bar of yet another London night club, ready to down a rare stiff drink on the house, when my inner voice intervened with a sudden pronouncement:

'Never go to Spain,' it strongly advised.

But here I am. In Nirvana. Bliss for some, a nightmare for others; for the sun shines on the just and wicked alike. And yet I can think of rather less beguiling confines back home in which to end one's days. A sense of humour could run into serious trouble in Edgware Road, for instance.

Besides, I have often veered from my keenest instincts, for perversity's sake.

The inner voice spoke again:

'If you *must* ignore the warning, you will damn well learn. The hard way.'

I surely inherit more than a measure of Celtic masochism, perhaps from my father's side of the family. Or in my case, could it be plain stupidity?

Moreover, it was in 1982 that I turned down a luxurious, easy to let apartment in Marbella in favour of a tatty old fisherman's cottage, east of Malaga. Tatty or not, it overlooked a delightful little beach with family boats, basking like insouciant seals in the evening sun.

With two fingers up in the direction of Marbella, and firmly pushing my dark voice into a safe corner, I concentrated on Maria's wide, magical eyes which said I should buy the house and be happy.

In twelve short days the Escritura, Copia Simple, was placed in my grateful hands, and I thanked God for looking kindly upon his wayward child, a mere musician.

For the first few years, I could scarcely wait to escape the pressures and complexities of life in the big city, and take off for yet another relaxed, liquid holiday.

Not that I was ever completely 'dry' in London. It was just that Bacardi & Coke doesn't quite taste the same in a Hoxton pub, nor are the measures anything more than an insult to an English alcoholic like me.

'I see you 'ave yer own bar, Tone.' The Guv'nor had spotted my bottle – whisky this time – tucked away down by the piano stool.

'Well, with the prices *you* charge, what can I do?

It would be years before the idea of putting a full-size concert grand in my little Spanish house would come into my mind; years before I'd turn the tiny place into an elegant bar with the sound of the sea complementing the distinctive tones of the Steinway; years before the bitch next door would gnaw at my business, life-style and very soul. I wish I could say just a few years remained free of all upsets and interruptions to my peace of mind. No such luck. They were but part of the great test of life. Would I pass it, with or without those flying colours? Or would I be punished, not necessarily by The Almighty, but by envious, fault-finding or wicked human beings, ever anxious to bring one down?

By the early 80s, my days of innocence had long gone, and I could hardly be dubbed a saint. Nevertheless, rightly or wrongly, I considered it time to enjoy some of the fruits of my continual labours. Would my little fisherman's cottage provide them, or did it already spell more trouble than I had either anticipated or wished for?

CHAPTER 20

Meanwhile, in London, music gigs continued unabated: studio sessions, night-clubs, pubs, and God knows what else.

In The Bacchus, Hoxton Street, I broke two rather nice pianos with my enthusiastic playing, and suggested we should look out for another.

'New piano, Tone?'

'Yes, Henry. I've broken these two.'

We studied each other's faces and wondered who'd be the first to burst into real laughter, and then be serious for a moment. But we held each other in tremendous respect. A sense of humour and a nose for business saved the day.

'Oh, come on, Henry,' I continued. 'You know the punters like to see me sweat and smash out the stuff. It's entertainment.'

'All very well, Tone,' he smiled. 'These pianos cost money.'

'But you only hire them... Look, if I lean on Markson's to let us have a really good one at a reduced hiring charge...'

'All right, Tone. All right. I know you do a bit of business with 'em yerself. We'll go 'un pick one out next week. How's Tuesday for you?'

'Fine. Thanks, Henry.' Who could wish for a better guv'nor?

The deal was struck, and though I still did not have a Steinway to work on, the new Schimmel upright did a marvellous job. Even I couldn't break it. And with a little bit of 'tweaking' with the woodwork and a good mike strategically placed inside, its tone remained sound and even. And all the while, double and treble vodkas were being clocked up on the till and downed in expansive, Cockney style. The punters continued to be happy and loud. But my band was louder... Who said the Spanish are the noisiest people on earth? Some say they take second place to the Japanese. Wonders never cease.

As if to add spice to the rough and tumble of playing in an East London environment, albeit with excellent musicians and an audience of colourful villains, pinned to the walls by my noisy band and a governor who stood no nonsense within those walls wherein he took "loads of money", my supplementary late-night residency in 14 Club in Piccadilly fitted the bill perfectly…

Gay is hardly the word here, for I would witness more fights with accompanying blood in that place than ever I'd see in the 'straight' Bacchus. Life is stranger than fiction, and I just kept playing… 'Don't shoot the piano player' is not an idle catch-phrase. But musicians are tough. We have to be, if we want to earn a living. Besides, all kinds of interesting people drifted into 14 Club between disturbances, and sat round the piano to imbibe and soak up the atmosphere: Robert Carrier and his friends, Helen Shapiro and hers, the late Jimmy Edwards, without his trombone, a couple of American bankers, seeking out pretty boys.

The club became a huge success, and it was time for it to be 'turned over'.

'You're going to have a visit, Jack,' I warned. The stronger of the two bosses looked at me with an incredulous eye.

'What do you mean, Tony?' he innocently questioned. I could not believe his naivety.

'Jack,' I went on. 'I'm only your piano player. But I'm a native of this town. We know about these things, my friend. Please get the police in before it happens.'

'Don't be silly, Tony. *Nothing's* going to happen.'

'Okay. Don't say I didn't warn you.'

About a week later, it happened. The place was turned over, chairs and tables went flying, blood was spilt, and the sex-change in the middle of her song issued her cool advice. 'Keep playing, Tony.' Luckily, I was hemmed in by the massive grand piano or rather the boudoir grand with a huge piano-shaped top, covering and extending the area to provide plenty of seating space for customers and their drinks. Needless to say, many of our more nervous clients had wisely fled. But I kept playing, as advised.

When the gang had left, we all breathed a sigh of relief and downed another drink.

'Well, Jack,' I said as we calmed down and considered the situation. 'Wasn't I right?'

'Unfortunately, yes. How did you know what would happen?' He gave me a measured look of inquiry, rather than total suspicion.

'Merely a smell for these things, Jack. I had no specific information, believe me. But listen, they'll come for *you*, next.'

'Don't be silly. That's the end of the matter.'

'You think so?'

A few days later, I was proved right again. Three beefy guys approached Jack and began to lash out. But Jack was fired up. Gay he might well have been; weak, no. He took them all on, and won. And peace reigned once more.

We all congratulated Jack for his toughness and resolve. He gave me a quizzical look of understanding 'Thanks for keeping the music going. I shall get the C.I.D. in tomorrow.'

And so he did. Once a policeman, always a policeman, they say. I could spot the plain-clothed guys and girls from the piano. The club settled down and blossomed into a happy venue for people of all proclivities and professions, and I felt confident enough to ask the outrageous Larry Lawson, an American pianist and crooner living in London, to deputize for me. The arrangement worked well, and we continued to give each other gigs and cover one another if, for any reason, either of us became 'incapable'... I, for one, have long prided myself on my capacity for alcohol – without, I hope, its affecting the quality of my work. But no one is infallible.

One uncompromising night, I was caught out quite unforgivably. Larry, bless him, stepped into the breach, as I would subsequently for him, on occasion. Arriving that evening at 14 Club, I lurched into the doorway, focusing nowhere, it seemed, and (God knows how) reached the piano around which sat an excited mob of young people, eager to hear some flashy stuff from 'Fingers' Sharp. I plumped down on the stool, gave them all a silly grin, and looked down at the keys which simply grinned back at me and refused to help. I could not tell which was which... In all my professional life, I had never suffered such an experience. But my friend Larry Lawson immediately recognized the problem, and offered to do the whole gig for me. So rare in his case, I thanked him and my lucky stars he was sober – for *that* night, at least.

We laughed about it afterwards; even the guv'nors, who took it all in their stride.

And still the gigs piled up. Some strange recording sessions also came my way, not least a session for a Tampax advert. Not to be sniffed at, folks. So I got down to some serious stuff on the piano. Shame, but I don't think the advertising company could quite accept the raunchy feel I'd produced, inspired by Eve Graham's excellent vocals and a splendid old Steinway grand. They were looking, understandably, for a somewhat smoother approach to back their client's product, and help cushion and romanticize the functional inconveniences of countless women.

Ah well, I still got paid. It was time to find the sun, and let the world go by.

CHAPTER 21

In the summer of '83, the little town of Nirvana began to boom. While Maggie reinstalled herself on her throne with a big majority in Westminster back home, English tourists here vied with each other to spend their own or anyone else's money in the best bars and restaurants on offer.

As for live music, even British-run bars were allowed a share, for the local authorities could not be seen to penalize too soon - at least until those Brits had firmly established themselves in positions of reluctant return to Blighty. They liked the sun. So hit 'em when they really start to spend money, and when they grow cocky. Bars and clubs run by ex-pats are easy pickings for the local 'Gestapo'. And in Nirvana, who needs lessons from another country on that point? Sunny Spain, it would seem, has never quite forgotten The Armada, and is compelled to compensate and punish the English for that unmitigated disaster.

But England's historic escape from invasion in 1588 could not have been further from my mind a few years later in 1983. With music gigs in London appearing secure and plentiful, I decided I could afford a month's holiday in my rough but – for me, if not for others – romantic little fisherman's house. So, in late September, I packed my bags and took off for Malaga.

Nirvana flowed with well-turned-out, elegant visitors, and one would never have imagined that in under twenty years the summer streets would fill with aggressive-looking, tattooed men and women and their cloned bullet-headed young. Their numbers, 'tis true, have visibly decreased in the passing years. Perhaps there's not enough for them to do in town. Nor perhaps are they prepared to shuffle along in sympathy with the Zimmer-frames, wheel-chairs or the odd walking stick. The image doesn't quite fit.

So, where have the beautiful people gone, and where are the educated tourists? Or are these bourgeois, even elitist concepts, bordering on the politically incorrect? Times change. But in '83, Nirvana was still natural Spain, able and willing to accept foreigners as long as they fitted in, and were not here to invade or disturb the indigenous way of life.

I had invited Bet to stay with me for the second half of my vacation. She had long been my favourite aunt. And now that I had a place on the Med, I instinctively desired to give her a holiday in belated gratitude for her care for me in those barmy days of yore. So often would she ply me with good food and a bed for the night, and listen to me practicing on her Steinway baby grand in part-preparation for my harpsichord recitals in The Purcell Room, London. I still believe she privately concurred with Sir Thomas Beecham's unanswerable description of the harpsichord. But aunt Bet remained discreet. Besides, my recitals were given on Thomas Goff instruments, arguably the most beautiful sounding harpsichords of their or any other time. And little did she know I'd one day own a full-size Steinway concert grand piano. It pleased her I took the opportunity to give her a free 'recital' on her baby grand.

On one such occasion she couldn't resist climbing on to the piano top, and dusting away like a crazy sketch on The Morecambe & Wise Show. 'How about it?' she said with a wry grin. Looking back on those days, I might well have been a great deal more successful if my agent had seen the joke and booked my aunt as part of the act.

Bet arrived on a fine October day, and immediately took to Nirvana. She liked the neatness of the place, the character and atmosphere, the love and care the locals showed for their children and houses; a gentle neighbour who welcomed her with a flower.

As something of an alcoholic, I welcomed her with a drink. 'Ah,' she gasped with pleasure. 'I needed that.'

The same evening, I conducted a blind test on her. For years she had enjoyed her Gordon's gin without complaint. Even she could not see which bottles I switched to put her off scent. A litre of Torres gin sold for one pound, Sterling in those days, or 200 Pesetas; Larios for 250; Gordon's for 300. A litre, remember.

'Well, what do you think?'

'This one,' she answered without hesitation. It's always a matter of taste, but Larios still know what they're doing, in Spain.

Bombay Sapphire is quite another matter, I feel. But my own taste-buds had yet to be developed, as far as gin was concerned. Whisky and brandy was another story.

After showering, and a quick change of clothes, we left the house and made for the restaurant. Bet exuded health and happiness, and if her skirt appeared a trifle on the short side for a woman of her age, who cared? She wanted to show her nephew what the 'old' folks could do. Old, be damned. She was stepping out like a young 'un.

We had soon reached the restaurant, already buzzing with activity and atmosphere as crêpes were tossed high in the sizzling pan by tall, handsome Paco, while his pretty Swedish wife Eva rattled away in several languages, and kept everyone happy at the bar.

With yet another large drink apiece, the smell of good cooking in our nostrils - herbs, spices, the whiff of a fine cigar, the glow on diners' faces as they spooned their delicious fish soup, the clink of wine glasses, the chatter and the laughter - Bet and I were more than ready to eat. Our taste-buds had been working overtime, and so it seemed had my aunt's bladder control. But control herself she did, and after a noticeable lurch down from her bar-stool (the waiter and I quickly preventing any serious damage), she walked through the restaurant with a delightful giggle, and began climbing the spiral staircase to the Ladies.

I looked on and prayed she would not fall. She had refused all assistance in the tricky operation, and either by a miracle or her own dogged determination she made it to the top. A seventy-six year old lady in a short skirt still has her pride. But Bet had always been a woman of guts and action. Even as a girl of sixteen, she was dashing around on a motor-bike and dating strongly, Victorian mother notwithstanding. She also had a personality and intelligence to match that determination. I loved her, and still do.

The descent from the Ladies, from where I was now sitting at the table, appeared a somewhat easier proposition than the ascent. I kept my fingers crossed in case I was wrong, or all too easily right. But with a wonderful smile stretching her worldly face, she descended with considerable grace, sat in a chair opposite me, and burst out laughing.

'Golly. I don't know how I made it,' she confessed. We laughed as I handed her a glass of house red, and with a no-nonsense clink we toasted each other warmly.

Between mouthfuls of pepper steak and sips of wine, fresh laughter erupted on our table – so much so that I sensed we were getting close to being thrown out on our ears - until we looked around the room to see our disposition infecting others for the better.

We arrived back at the house, put on the lights, and went out on to the patio overlooking the beach.

'Oh, Tony, I do hope you manage to keep this place.'

'So do I. I shall do my damnedest, never fear.'

'I'm sure you will.'

I went back inside and re-emerged with two glasses, ice, lemons, a bottle of Bacardi, and cokes. 'Have you tried this?' I asked, pointing to the fat bottle of clear white liquid – 350 pesetas in those days. 'Never,' she said with a smile. 'Now, Tony. Not too much.' She already knew my idea of a good drink.

With her attention momentarily diverted towards the sea, I poured two large measures, and topped up with coke to disguise the fact. To my surprise and delight, she downed hers with no trouble at all, and with remarkable speed. Maybe it was the robust meal we'd eaten or the sound of the sea that encouraged her, or perhaps my own pace of consumption.

I refilled our glasses with Bacardi and added some coke while we continued to chat about anything and everything: family, hopes and fears, the meaning of life, the state of the world, the pursuit of happiness.

Time passed, and I made ready to re-pour.

'No you don't, Tony. I've had quite enough, thank you. It was lovely… I think I'll turn in for the night. I'm feeling a little tired now. I'm seventy-six, you know.'

'And you're marvellous.' I gave her a wee hug. 'Now, remember,' I went on, 'you're supposed to be on holiday. So you don't have to get up at the crack of dawn.'

She smiled, and got up from her easy chair. But as she began to walk along the patio, back towards the house, she found herself caught off balance. With commendable assurance she recovered. 'You *bugger*,' she said, turning round to face me - still sitting there, knowing full well the effect my alcoholic offerings would no doubt have on her, 'I'll *get* you in the morning. You and your **MACARI**.'

At about 7.30 next morning, my misty eyes glimpsed the light across the water through the open window of my room, and a familiar face grinning at me as I lay in bed. ''Mornin',' it said with youthful perkiness. 'What shall we do, today?'

My God. Was there no limit to this wonderful, crazy woman's energy? Needless to say, despite all protestations on my part, before the morning had hardly begun she was down on her knees – scrubbing and cleaning the tiles, washing the bathroom, putting the kitchen shipshape, sorting the pots and pans, and God knows what else. 'Get out of my way,' she snapped with a good-humoured grin etched across her face.

After lunch, she was down into the sea for a relaxing swim. And then she lay on the beach and sunned herself while the waves crashed over the rocks, and a fisherman mended his net.

Later that week, my aunt prepared our first meal at home. While I busied myself under the shower, she suddenly noticed an odd burning smell, and turned to witness high up on the wall a bare wire, happily in the process of eating its way along to the bathroom where I was still showering.

'Tony. Quick. The house is on fire.'

I put a towel round myself, stepped out on to the floor, and walked into the room as nonchalantly as I felt appropriate. After all, "when in Rome" and all that.

'Well, *do* something,' she urged.

'Oh, don't worry,' I said with an even voice. 'It'll burn itself out in a minute.'

'It'll burn the *house* down, you fool. How can you be so calm?'

Providence must have been on my side, yet again. For before I could answer my aunt (supposing I'd had anything constructive to say), the fire went out as suddenly as it had apparently started. 'Well, what *now*?' she pressed.

'What now? It's stopped, hasn't it?'

Her mouth fell open at my casualness and lack of concern.

'You can't just leave it.'

'Why not?' I teased. 'All right. I'll get an electrician when I've finished in the bathroom.'

She shook her head in disbelief. But I was determined to impress upon her that in Andalucia, people tend not to panic in these situations.

'Blimey, I wish I could be like you,' she sighed as we began our first course of leek soup which she'd immaculately prepared and served at the table in my tiny, all-purpose sitting-room. I grinned and poured the wine.

Within the hour, Bautista, the local electrician banged on our door. He walked in with his young nephew who seemed somewhat confused and resentful of being dragged along during The Feria, to see his uncle mend a stupid Englishman's wiring system. But I *wasn't* a stupid Eng... I'm not complaining.

Bautista climbed up on his ladder, and began to work. In under half an hour the job was 'done'. Bare wires sprouted everywhere, and Heath Robinson would have been proud. But I was happy. This was still old-fashioned Spain, and my street was old. How else would I have been able to purchase my lovely little wreck, if it were not for Maria who ran the street like a Mini-Mafia? She was an illiterate but intelligent gypsy woman with bags of drive and personality and whose eyes would invariably rumble the phoney. I had obviously made a hit with her, and that's why she had told all other interested parties that the house had been sold, despite the notice SE VENDE clearly displayed in the front window. She wanted *me* to have it.

How we all mourned her untimely death from cancer in her mid-Forties.

And then things would change. For the moment, I savoured simple Spain – with a little help from Scotland. Happily I poured out large measures of Chivas Regal and an orange for the boy. 'Gracias, Bautista. Quanto?'

He held up one finger to indicate a thousand pesetas. 'Suficiente,' he said with a smile. I gave him his money, adding 500 for his nephew and for what might be left of The Feria for the day.

'El whisky es bueno, Tony.'

'Thank good old Scotland for that, Bautista, and my aunt who bought it.'

As time rushed by, I became anxious Bet should enjoy her short holiday to the full. But she seemed quite happy to soak up the atmosphere of Nirvana itself. We indulged ourselves at several choice restaurants and bars, and joined in the fun on the last days of The Feria. Dismissing most of the available tourist excursions, we settled for a trip to Granada. Of course, this was all before the days of motorways, relative comfort, and speed. We caught the bus by the main roadside of Nirvana early one morning, and broke the journey with an arranged 'breakfast' at a kind of mountain café. Serenaded with some decidedly dodgy guitar-playing from an old man, specially commissioned, it seemed, to squeeze the last ounce of patient humour and a few more pesetas from the breakfasting English, we were glad to board that bus again, and be on our way.

But it was all worth it, especially the tour of The Alhambra: a wonder to behold. For even the thought of Medieval throats being cut after dinner by a jealous king scarcely detracts from an appreciation of fine arches, delicate pillars and exquisite alabaster carving for which the Moors are deservedly famous. If one *has* to die here, it could hardly happen in a more inspirational setting.

The holiday was all too quickly over. And as our plane climbed above the mountains stretched out below us, my aunt uttered a sigh of fulsome yearning – a collage of visions and emotions too broad and yet too deep to express in words. Bet had always been a woman in whose company there were no awkward gaps. The strength of character and intelligence emanating from her was enough to satisfy her companion in any quiet moment. Her love did the rest. A special aunt indeed.

'Have you enjoyed the holiday?' I ventured unnecessarily.

'Very much,' she answered softly. 'I don't suppose I'll see this again in my life-time.'

Yet somehow I knew damn well she would.

CHAPTER 22

The months passed by. All that winter I worked bloody hard, and looked forward to Spring.

At last it arrived. Eagerly I packed my bags, and flew out again to Malaga, travelling alone. On this holiday I would not have the pleasure of my aunt's company, but at least I'd have a clean house in which I could relax, and perhaps do a spot of writing.

For some odd reason, the fact I'd let the house to a friend of a friend during my absence did not worry me unduly, despite my initial misgivings. I had been assured of the man's reliability, cleanliness, and sensitivity towards Maria and all the good people of the street, and that he would leave the house as he found it. Bet had done a wonderful job, and it did not cross my mind for one moment that I'd find it in any other than a reasonable condition. 'Don't worry,' the man had said. 'I'll look after Maria. After all, she has an *enormous* respect for you.'

On arrival at Malaga I decided to take a taxi all the way to the house. Why not? The gigs had been plentiful. I could afford it, at least for once.

The car journey proved to be very pleasant, and I enjoyed practicing my new-found if short-lived 'fluency' in the Andalucian dialect where words run into each other, and all the ends are cut off. So what? Language is a living tool of communication. For people.

Ah, Nirvana. As we turned the corner into my sweet calle, I felt nothing could disturb my well-earned equilibrium. The taxi-driver had been great fun, and in generous spirit I gave him a good tip and bade him farewell. It was a glorious afternoon. And I was home again.

The most I expected to do the first day would be to throw open the doors and windows and get out the broom for a light-hearted, easy sweep round. I could then relax and begin to enjoy the holiday.

Happily I turned the key to my door. But as I stepped inside, an indescribable spectacle greeted me and stunned my senses… I froze in horror… For in abject disbelief, I staggered and stumbled on through a house I could no longer feel to be my own…

Everywhere I looked, the 'alterations' were so complete and apparently irreversible that my natural anger replaced itself with bursts of barely controlled hysteria. Nothing that had happened to another aunt's house in London after a V2 attack in World War 2 could, to my mind, compare at that moment with what was splayed out before me: damage and filth screamed and leered at me from every angle. And to think the man had been highly recommended and... *Where* had my whicker chairs gone and my rocker and..? The *bastard*... My eyes were drawn to the once-loved Andalucian fire-place, now entirely scorched to the ceiling, and below – to the huge pile of ashes which could only have been the molecular reductions of the furniture that was once mine.

I glanced at the walls, hoping *something*, at least, had escaped the ravages of the madman's hand. But the nightmare continued. Every wall had been gashed – whereupon I presumed he'd nailed his God-dam paintings. I walked into the main bedroom, and lifted the sheets on my bed. Jesus. The original colours were barely recognizable.

I'd seen enough. And closing my eyes, I appealed to God and anyone else who may have been listening, and tried to convince myself that all I'd witnessed had merely been a twisted illusion or temporary though serious aberration of my mind, and that when I opened my eyes again everything would be as we'd left it in October. How I yearned for time to reverse itself and take another, happier path.

Yet, as my blood began to boil up again, I knew, alas, this was for real, and that I'd been dealt an unkind and unwarranted insult. In vain I searched in my memory for an equivalent experience, just so I could feel I was not, after all, beginning to hallucinate or embrace complete madness after years of loose, wild living. But I could find nothing comparable. In childhood I had, like most of us, suffered more than one bad dream, and as I grew up, life itself provided its own nightmares, most of which could somehow be contained within a framework of probability, predictability, or just deserts. *This* was different. Quite different.

When at last courage and righteous anger joined forces to open my eyes again, I found myself standing in half an inch of dust and grime, and gazing forlornly at a rug whose original pattern and colouring had been disfigured and distorted with generous coatings of crude oil. Surely the torture would end soon if I just held on? All things, even the bad, must perish in time.

And so it came to pass that I foolishly believed, despite everything I'd seen, that the little guest bedroom, at least, would be spared. After all, there had only been him and perhaps the occasional slut to keep him company. I opened the bedroom door. What a dreamer I'd been... My eyes alighted upon my favourite bedside chair. Yes, incredibly, though the main shape appeared intact, its legs had ignominiously been chopped 'down to size' so that it now stood lowly, gelded, and like me, bloody angry. I felt for that chair. And then I found a hammer, and prayed he would appear, so that I might calmly but firmly crush his skull, and gladly serve life.

CHAPTER 23

The years rolled on. And for the most part they turned out to be unexpectedly pleasant, for the shock of the 'alterations' at the hands of an American madman had, naturally, put me on my guard. I was not anxious to precipitate another such event. Life and people would do more of their tricks in due course. I had only to be patient. My intention was to relax and enjoy my special sanctuary whenever I could, and in my own way.

My livelihood continued to flourish in my home town of London where I'd always felt comfortable. Not that I could afford to live there nowadays.

In the late 80s, the great boom pervaded the city for a while, and I sensed I'd have to cram in the gigs before the bubble burst. With the collapse of the gay piano bar in Piccadilly (The London Electricity Board, not known for sympathy towards minority groups, wanted their premises back), I was compelled to find another late-night spot to 'double-up' my job at The Bacchus. A quick phone call produced a residency at The Eve Club in Regency Street. I would merely be the pianist in someone else's band, but what the hell? It was a job. And there on stage sat a lovely old Blüthner boudoir grand to play on. So agreeable was its sound and action that I had little difficulty in extracting one of London's best piano players from his boring top musical to deputize for me an hour each Friday night while I played at The Bacchus.

I could never describe The Eve Club gig as 'heavy'. Compared with my times as band-leader in The Celebrity Club or more particularly The New Embassy where that 'first degree' murder took place while I played on with my trio, I'd view The Eve Club more as a mad-hatter's tea party. It would be a wonder any of these clubs exist today. The world changes, drink and drive laws prevail, and then there is the question of sheer expense, disease, and plain damned boredom. For us musicians, boredom could be relieved by a bloody great row in the 'green-room' between sets. I, for one, love to argue about politics. So I used to encourage a 'mild' skirmish over a whisky or two... The bass player at The Eve Club thought he had me in his sights. But I'd keep the argument going, for fun. Back on stage, the tension between us could be cut with a knife: it made for a very lively set...

Yet the man, bless his heart, still ran me back to my flat in his car. Perhaps he wouldn't wish to be reminded.

It was time to move on. In 1988 I clinched a residency at a newly-launched restaurant in London called China Jazz. The idea of good Chinese food and 'cocktail' jazz I suppose was fairly new at the time, and I eagerly took up the challenge. One can book the best musicians in London, and though two days in each week on the phone to such end can be a bit of a bind, it's always a pleasure for a musician to be among the top notches.

The question of the piano was settled very quickly and efficiently.

'Jump in the car, Tony,' said the boss. Off we zoomed down the road in his Bentley, once more to Markson's.

'No, we haven't a Steinway for you,' bleated Julian Markson. 'But look, the Yamaha C3 will do perfectly well. Try it.'

Quietly sighing again, I sat down to the piano. 'Well, not bad, I must admit. But...'

'Tony. Let's settle for this, now. I promise I'll go with you to Steinway's once the restaurant is running well. Whether I'll be able to persuade my partner is another matter.'

'Okay, James.' My desire for a Steinway Grand would have to be put on the back burner yet again. I would get what I wanted one day, by hook or by crook.

At least the money for the job was decent. And a first-class Chinese meal on the house each night could not be dismissed out of hand. Most of my musos were happy to have the gig, and though I was personally put under considerable pressure by the management, an hour's drinking at a good Young's pub in the break with the lads made a world of difference.

Before the year was out, I had persuaded the boss to come to Steinway Hall and listen to the top quality stuff. After all, he enjoyed his long wheelbase Bentley. And his second car, a Porche 928S, sat gleaming outside in the street. Surely, he'd appreciate the real thing as soon as he'd heard it...

Already seated at a brand new baby grand Model M from the Hamburg factory, I idled over the keys, picking out beautiful notes in a well-known ballad. As James entered the showroom, his eyes popped out of his head with delight and amazement. He had never before heard a Steinway played live; and so close at hand. The head salesman whose own old Steinway Concert Grand

I would buy, years later, stood deferentially by the piano and waited for James's first words.

'I want one,' he could see forming in his eyes if not on his lips... 'I've never heard such a beautiful sound,' he finally said.

'Well, there you are, James,' I offered. 'You have a Porche and a Bentley. You get what you pay for.'

Had I done it this time? Had I finally convinced someone he should provide bloody old Tony Sharp a Steinway? Or would Sharp have to wait and allow life's twists and turns to relinquish one to him at last?

With a quick swallow at the price of the new baby grand I'd been playing, James's flexible mind slid into the next step up, and he moved over to a Boudoir, Model O. 'How much more is *this* one?'

Don't go too far, James, I thought. My mind was racing, too. Or we'll never get one for the restaurant. I had a distinct feeling James's Chinese partner would put a block on it, even though the soon-to-be-opened Jazz Café a few doors from China Jazz would not hesitate to buy a Steinway Grand. But then, the Chinese have their limitations, like anyone else. Ying Tong, Ying Tong, Twiddle my Toe (or its 'variations') hardly demands the nuances of an expensive piano. Needless to say, I did not get what I wanted.

'Stick with the Yamaha a little longer, Tony. After all, some of the top musicians are using them now.'

'Really?' I growled under my breath, not least for the sly inference that I was not in the league of a top musician. Oh, how people *love* names.

But I soon forgot the hurtful remark, and concentrated on booking some damned good musos for the gig. Besides, the bosses at China Jazz hardly knew their arse from their elbow when it came to music. Like most managements who only see 'pounds, shillings and pence', they would never really know the joy music-making can give a musician, whilst remaining envious of that inherent and, for them, elusive gift.

Yet, I still thank them for a whole year's employment, during which time I had fun, booking Chris Lawrence, Dudley Phillips, Simon Woolf, Alec Dankworth, Jeff Clyne and Mario Castronari on string bass, to name but a few first-rate players, together with Paul Carmichael, Patrick Bettison and the ever popular and busy session player Steve Pearce on bass guitar. Even *I* was not so mad as to book them all for the same night, though the concept must have crossed my mind once or twice – perhaps over a whisky or two.

My regular drummer was the late Bill Eyden, who swung like mad and remained a delight to work with. Jazzers might well remember the late Tubby Hayes with whom Bill worked for a time as well as hanging out with some pretty wild rock bands. Unlike yours truly, who wore his bitterness rather badly at times, one never seemed to catch Bill with a heavy heart, though he had much to complain about. The general public can still hear Bill, playing drums on the classic 'A Whiter Shade of Pale' for which he received the princely sum of twenty pounds. *His* decision.

Other drummers graced the portals of China Jazz when I ran the band: Tony Kinsey, Brian Abrahams, John Dillon and Clarke Tracey (son of Stan), amongst others.

Even in this Spanish "back-water", I occasionally bump into the odd sax player who remembers the histrionics of China Jazz during my time there: Alan Barnes seems to recall those days with *some* affection. Then there was Mark Ramsden, Martin Speake and the brilliant session player Jamie Talbot.

The long list of female singers, willing to add their voice and influence to the proceedings included the pretty Sue Shattock, the smooth, mellifluous Claire Martin with whose boyfriend I got drunk after another gig of mine (we finished a bottle of Wild Turkey between us, and Claire just *knew* her young man had been in my company, and fetched the police). There was also the powerful Jill Manly, and her powerful, 'manly' voice, and one night I booked a favourite of mine: Jackie Rawe, though *her* speciality was *funk,* rather than jazz. Nevertheless, she seemed to turn on even the Chinese boss – in more ways than one. Besides, I think he preferred funk to jazz, without knowing why.

I needed another holiday. That winter, I decided to fly away for a two-week break in Nirvana.

Arriving in good humour at the house, I turned the key in the lock and opened the front door. Ah,.. just as I'd left it. No need for more than the usual sweep-round, and I could enjoy myself.

I put down my bags in the hallway, and walked along the passage to the patio. The swish of the sea was already producing its unfailing balming of my senses. Home again and numb to the nasty things of life, I thanked God for the blessing and wished for little more. But as I turned my head from the balcony over the beach, I spotted it: a hideous monstrosity, a great ugly wall with sharp green glass sticking out at irregular angles, challenging anyone foolish enough to attempt a climb. At least a quarter of my superb view had been blocked, brutalized by an insensitive mean-heart next door. The wall had been built in my absence, with not a care for feelings, aesthetics or neighbourliness.

As unwelcome anger rose in me once again, I wondered how best I could reverse this insult to my person and finer feelings, and devote the remainder of my short holiday to well-earned recreation and the writing of a few more short stories. But time was of the essence. I had to move fast.

'Go to The Town Hall,' suggested my local bank manager confidently, 'and they will send a policeman.' Fat chance anything will result from that, I thought.

With the arrival of a decidedly disinterested policeman who advised me to find out whether my neighbour had obtained the necessary permission for the construction of the wall, and then at least three futile visits to The Town Hall, I knew for sure my efforts to extract justice or even an explanation would be thwarted. *Someone* had been paid off, and Tony Sharp would just have to resort to plain old-fashioned violence. I have often wondered why so many people shy at the notion of a straightforward eye for an eye, seeing that they find Christ's more sophisticated teachings too difficult to follow.

Down would come the wall. I quickly contacted a couple of English 'heavies' who hesitated to do the job. When I said 'Think it over. But if you don't, I'll get someone who will', they thought it over. 'We'll do it,' was the prompt answer. They needed the money.

It was a hell of a job. Great steel girders had been implanted to fix it to the existing 'party' wall. The base proudly boasted of an impregnation of hard flint-stone to strengthen it even further, and the men had little space in which to work. As one of them bravely hacked away at it, standing on the narrow precipice overlooking the beach, we roped him in as best we could.

Could he do it, without killing himself? The wind blew hard, and his feet began to slip as he worked. And all the while, not a few inquisitive spectators and a couple with walkie-talkies looked on.

The wind blew anew, and I had to make a decision. 'Just level it off, Keith,' I said. 'As long as I have my view back, she can keep the bloody base.' To be responsible for the death of a man in order to achieve a perfect restoration was not in my book of civilized behaviour.

Little did I know the bitch would use that base to form a triangle into which more earth, cacti and a grotesque bush would be installed. My original view would disappear once again.

But for the time being, 'la vista' had re-materialized before my eyes, and the 'war' had begun. Despite the mess the men had made which would doubtless lead to acrimony, I paid them the agreed money and gave them each a stiff whisky.

'Shall we drop our card through her front door?' one of them cheekily suggested. This putting up and knocking down walls could be quite lucrative... 'You dare,' I grinned. With handshakes and dry smiles all round, they left, no doubt to have a few more beavies in a local bar, and discuss their latest demolition job.

Even at that stage, I felt 'The Wall' episode would one day make a good story. But for the moment I contented myself with a succinct note which I popped through her front door. It read:

> *Dear Helga,*
> *You can see The Wall is down. Should another appear, I shall do exactly the same...*
> *I do hope we can get back to being good neighbours...*

In the summer of the following year, I took another break to Nirvana – when my neighbour happened to be in residence at the same time.

What the hell? I knocked on her door, and with the usual greetings over, I explained my behaviour. The Wall had been more than a blot on the 'landscape', as far as I was concerned. I could not concentrate on writing my short stories. Why didn't you contact me in London so that we could work out a solution of your security worries in an equitable and artistic way? I was sorry to appear so violent, but that ugly wall *had* to come down.

'We too were very angry,' she said. Yet remarkably, she calmed down as I proceeded to suggest the construction of something acceptable to both sides.

But she had already made up her mind to plant the cacti… and more.

CHAPTER 24

As most of us know to our cost, the recession which hit the UK with such magnitude in the early 90s became a much more prolonged and stressful period than the previous 'blip' of '81. For The Falklands War of 1982 brought Maggie bouncing back with her big majority in the summer of the following year. British confidence grew, and in a whirlwind of forceful government, Arthur Scargill was put to the test and resoundly beaten. The unions were knocked off their 'unassailable' perches, ruthless bosses had their way once more, and Maggie thrived on her own diet of elected dictatorship.

When I voted for her, I was condemned and lampooned by my fellow musicians as a fascist. Why should I care? I was producing more gigs for them than most of them were for me. As long as I pleased the people who paid me, I cared not what people said about me. Talk is cheap and easy. It's not so easy to persuade bosses to loosen the purse-strings for mere musicians. But as they say: some people have it, others do not.

In any case, musicians, like actors, are used to being in and out of work. We don't necessarily moan like a good honest miner or factory worker who after thirty or forty odd years of solid employment, finds himself redundant. That's bad enough. But who ever heard of proper redundancy money for musicians? In England? Some of us even have families to feed.

GIG means GOD IS GOOD, because we are lucky enough to hook a 'one night stand'; a residency is an out and out luxury.

Yet for many, the 90s recession matched the 30s crash. If fewer people actually threw themselves from tall buildings in their distress, a vast number went bust and had to think on their feet – for their immediate rather than long-term survival.

As for us musos, well.., when villains begin to tighten their money-belts, we swallow hard and look for the life-boat, whilst the 'lucky' ones in top musicals wonder when the show will close or whether they can ever trust a 'dep' not to pinch their 'chairs'.

Even my residency at 'Rifles', in Enfield, was about to collapse. It was a gig where the guv'nors, it had first appeared, were richer yet than my friend Henry at The Bacchus, and they had asked me to put together a funky band – as opposed to the China Jazz sound. This I did, proceeding to enjoy many a 'session' there with some great guys such as Steve Pearce on bass guitar and Steve Sanger on drums. It was at 'Rifles', one Christmas, I think, where the naughty Wild Turkey episode occurred – with Ian Harrison, vocalist and Wild Turkey drinker for *one* night. His then girlfriend, Claire Martin, I was informed, made him promise to steer clear of the stuff and, no doubt, to be extra careful of that wicked Tony Sharp.

But the recession deepened, and with my back squarely pushed to the wall, I prepared for the worst.

'You'll just have to sell that little place in Spain, won't you?' How could the new, strict bank manager know to what extent Tony Sharp's guile would stretch? How could he foresee that bloody Tony Sharp would keep not only the little place in Spain, but also his minute flat in central London, do a deal with the same bank, and years later buy and sell the London flat to his neighbours, and with the money open a piano bar in his Spanish house?

I am not gloating, for destiny would ensure an extremely stressful time for me in dear old Nirvana. I had been warned.

But in the summer of '92, a plane took off from Gatwick, and rose higher and higher in the sky towards Malaga with yours truly on board.

Wonderful Christopher Orlebar, our captain for the journey, had, before take-off, invited me up into the cockpit to see the flight. He already possessed a copy of my first fantasy novel, and I in turn had attempted to comprehend his book 'The Concorde Story'. We had soon sealed a huge respect for each other, and a shared sense of humour augured a lasting friendship.

After allowing me to enjoy more than half the flight on deck, his co-pilot asked me if I'd like to see the landing. I thanked him and quickly accepted. But I was ready for that stiff whisky. Back in the cabin I sank a couple of large ones, and returned to the cockpit.

Sitting bolt upright in the seat behind the captain and co-pilot, they safely strapped me in. From there I observed the calm and seemingly uneventful but fascinating descent and landing. We had arrived.

Warmly wishing Christopher and his co-pilot all the best for the future, and with formalities and baggage collection over, I finally emerged into the welcome sunshine a happy man. A rather nice 'Bienvenido' to full-time living in Spain, I thought.

But officially, I had come to sell my house. Would I do it? Would I, hell… Going through the motions of a sale, so to speak, I wrote to the new bank manager in England and informed him of the position. 'I think it would be far better,' I said perhaps somewhat unkindly, 'to stay in Spain and look for work.'

Now, I should hate to feel I could ever be responsible for losing a bank manager his job. But when one's back is to the wall, one fights. In the midst of a recession it's every man for himself.

So, after playing a few numbers on a Hohner electric piano (do they make them any smaller? Honda, perhaps?) I was offered a tentative gig in an English-run restaurant. For tentative it transpired to be. Elevated to the position of third partner in the business, I waited upon the inevitable. Within two weeks the restaurant was closed.

Here we go again, I thought. I should have listened to the hit man in the Caribbean who had unequivocably enunciated his philosophy… 'I couldn't live like you, Tony.., scratching around for gigs.' How could I forget what he had said? 'I live like a King.' One might find the odd king, from time to time, but hit men are rarely known for their musical skills. In any case, the *Big Boys* don't dirty their own hands.

With my tail between my legs, I ambled up to 'The Old Cellar' restaurant which was run by a very enterprising Spaniard called Mr Table, or

Pepe Mesa in Spanish. He had previously offered me six nights a week in his restaurant just before he opened the business. But I had turned him down, not ungraciously, I trust, with the announcement of my 'partnership' in an English restaurant. How stupid could I be?

Perhaps Pepe knew such an arrangement could not last, and that my foolish ego would lead to disaster. In the meantime he had put his young son into employment - playing the piano a couple of nights a week. I was then given three and later four nights a week, and swallowed my pride as best I could.

As it turned out, the gig developed into a very agreeable arrangement despite the piano I was required to work on, and I proceeded to entertain not only the customers but the powerfully-built chef, Antonio, who a year later and on several subsequent occasions would willingly lend his considerable weight and strength in the moving of my own, heavy piano from place to place.

I've long held a theory that if you make people laugh, you can have practically anything. There's more than a seed of truth in the old adage "Laugh, and the world laughs with you. Weep, and you weep alone".

In 1993, I was approached with a proposition which at first sight appeared to be the answer to my local ambitions: a partnership in a brand new piano bar. Would this be my chance at last to get my hands on a Steinway Grand? I recalled what my old friend Rowland Civil had said during a pub gig he had procured for me back in London: 'I have an old Steinway Concert Grand in dad's studio, doing nothing. If you find a buyer for me, there's a 'grand' in it for you.'

With a bit of luck, maybe his unwitting pun on the word 'grand' would eventually materialize into the reality of my dreams. Could I be asking for the moon? Little did I know at the time that Rowland's piano would one day be mine. God indeed moves in mysterious ways.

CHAPTER 25

In 1993 Nirvana witnessed the opening of a real piano bar with a fine acoustic instrument. My partner had eagerly taken up the idea of 'shipping' across Rowland's old concert grand. I in turn had twisted my friend's arm into allowing us to hire the piano for three months – on the strict understanding that one of us would buy the beast on the fourth month, or return it, intact, to England.

But it was agreed that I should have first refusal to buy. Would I ever find the money? Would I survive the partnership, or ignominiously be kicked out – with the piano sitting there in the 'local' to which I was legally connected?

Thus began the saga of the Steinway. It is an incredible story. Sadly, it is all true. But I am a survivor, and here (just) to tell the tale…

We waited on the top road where the buses from Malaga stop; waited and waited for the lorry that would deliver the Steinway to Nirvana.

As we stood, my partner and I, anxious that nothing should go wrong, a flash-back invaded my mind of the scene in 'High Noon' where Gary Cooper waits on tenterhooks for the noon train that would spell death to someone else, if not to him.

Peter and I were hardly expecting a posse of fearless bandits on this outing, but we did expect a few men adept at moving pianos in a professional way. The driver of the lorry (a huge articulated Volvo) and his young lad were friendly enough, but scarcely cut out for this task. To give Peter his due, he proved quick to improvise and rustle up several strong helpers and a dust-cart on which to transfer the Steinway.

The police refused a welcome to the lorry. It just would not be allowed access to the tiny, narrow streets of Nirvana.

So, onto the dust-cart the Steinway was raised and lowered: Volvo to dust-cart. A shameful omen, perhaps. But there it was.

While Peter and I steadied the piano, and raced through the unsuspecting streets of Nirvana, I encouraged him to relax and have some fun out of the proceedings. The lifting of our right arms in the Nazi salute while grinning at each other like naughty schoolboys drew some curious looks from some as well as the expected grimaces of disapproval from others. Nevertheless, I had high hopes our partnership would develop into a fun enterprise.

When the piano had been installed in the bar, and 'shod' so as to stand on the floor at the correct height, Peter, his wife and I celebrated the event with the clink of glasses, and…

It was then that I made my unfortunate suggestion. 'Look, you're a fine-looking man, Peter. Why don't you dress up in SS uniform? You'd look *fantastic*.'

There was no reaction for a second or two, and I wondered whether Peter had temporarily gone deaf as a result of all the excitement and dashing around, or had conveniently (and sadly, as far as I'm concerned) forgotten about our naughty Nazi salutes. Then suddenly, his hands and arms began to shake and grip the bar-top in anger, and his face took on the expression of one of those old thermometers we had in our East London back gardens after The Second World War. You could actually see the needle rise to 80 degrees Fahrenheit or more in the summer if you watched carefully, rare weather permitting.

With a quivering yet heated voice, Peter announced: 'My father spent the *whole* of the war, hiding from the Germans.'

I was not to be put off that easily. 'Yes,' I replied with English nonchalance. 'I'm sorry about that. We as Londoners didn't have such a good time, either. Nevertheless, I think you'd look *fantastic* in SS uniform.'

The last vestiges of shared humour had sadly disappeared for good, it seemed, and I was lucky to get home in one piece that day.

Despite the early blip in the relationship, albeit most significant, we just *had* to make the venture work. And so it did. It was a great success. Then very soon, no doubt because of its success, all sorts of strange people began to crawl out of the woodwork and edge their way into the business... Another member of my partner's family appeared on the scene, and then another – until finally, I blew up.

Many people commend me for my patience. And of course this is always gratifying to hear. But there are times, I openly admit, when the fuse is found to be somewhat short, and my strange bloods are set free. Needless to say, my partner took full advantage of this 'wee' explosion, and promptly put me on ordinary wages. I was sacked from the business while he looked around for another piano player.

It was now a game of cat and mouse, or perhaps cat and cat. Who would be top cat? I know I possess a cruel streak in my nature, but I try to keep this under lock and key until the need arises to release it. I much prefer to live peacefully and with equanimity. But if war is declared, then I shall fight in my own way. Beware. You will not know where I'm coming from.

Why should I have a conscience about this? After all, if you cross someone in London, comeuppance will surely be served upon you some day. Strangely, too many expats here in Nirvana consider themselves free of such an inconvenient fate. When comeuppance comes their way, someone else, naturally, is to blame. Life for us all is a hard lesson.

While my former partner and his wife continued their plotting, I hid my anger as best I could, and bided my time. Meanwhile, a new man was drawn into the business, innocently parting with a tidy sum of money which somehow got lost or simply melted away into infinity. Thank God I had not raised money to do the same, for I was watching my partner all the way. In this instance, at least, I had wisely swum along in tandem with my instincts, and held masochism at bay. I would have enough knocks in due course.

As the gig ran on a while longer, I called upon my psychic powers to come to my aid. They did not disappoint. I would be thrown out of the bar as soon as the new piano player was available.

'Buy the piano,' said my inner voice… But how would I find the money?

'I'll lend you the money,' piped another voice, in human form. It was the man whose money had 'mysteriously' disappeared. 'I have enough left over to cover your piano. *Anything* to spike those bastards.' My God, the venom had begun to flow. And this was my chance to buy the Steinway and begin a new gig somewhere else.

'Thanks a million, mate.' What a weight off my shoulders.

But now the real eruptions would break out. My former partner and his wife just could not believe an 'impecunious' piano player would find the money to buy a Steinway, how ever old the instrument might be.

Frantic phone calls were made across the water to Rowland Civil in London. Rowland, thank The Lord, made himself unavailable, and abided by our original agreement that I should have first refusal to buy. In red hot anger on the part of my 'partner' and his wife, I was promptly thrown out of the 'local'. But they still kept the Steinway.

Next move: how could I retrieve my property? My new lawyer gave me clear, unequivocal advice. 'Go in and get your piano as soon as possible.'

But the lock on the 'local' had been changed, and two large guard dogs had been installed to keep Tony Sharp out. I approached an English locksmith who agreed to fix the lock on condition my papers were in order and legitimate. They were.

We agreed on the money for the job, but the silly bugger grassed on me, and blew the whole thing.

Peter and his wife arrived at the bar to witness a posse of men, waiting to remove my piano. 'You're wasting your time, Tony,' said Peter with a smirk as I stood with my lawyer in the front doorway, and the men wondered what would be my next trick. As the door was shut in our faces, I quietly assured the guys I would not give up. With their agreement to try again, my lawyer and I set off to make a denuncia of The Piano Bar.

But the really effective turning point came with the timely help of a French lady-friend who introduced me to a firm of Spanish locksmiths. A meeting was arranged, and my papers meticulously scrutinized in the little shop of a decidedly serious Spaniard.

'Problema, amigo?' I innocently asked.

'No, no.' He pulled out his 'badge' from his trouser pocket. "Guardia Civil" was clearly marked. So I hadn't come to any old locksmith.

'Bueno, bueno,' I enthused. I just knew I was more than half-way there. My piano would surely be retrieved.

I chose a Sunday morning. 7a.m. to be precise. My men quietly gathered near the premises. A strong trailer drew up, and backed, making ready to receive its load. The locksmith arrived, and without fuss proceeded with his trade. And while my former partner's two sons, who had been drinking heavily the night before, dreamt of lovely things upstairs, the lock was removed and replaced, and my men and I entered the 'local' and began our task.

We removed the glass top, lightly fitted to protect the surface of the piano lid, and carefully placed it against a wall. All I wanted was my property. No more. Then after removing the pedal mechanism, we turned the piano over on to a large mattress and removed the legs as quietly as possible... 'Shush. Don't wake the boys.' Some muffled giggling, and on with the job.

Being a bit of a perfectionist, I would prefer we had left the premises with every bar-stool in its former neat position. A half-ton Steinway spirited away from the middle of an otherwise undisturbed room would surely be a dramatic and unnerving phenomenon to witness on first sight. But understandably, we were somewhat in a hurry.

As my huge piano was finally loaded and driven away, with the men making their way round the corner to my new venue, I thanked and paid the locksmith, and left with my friend who had lent me the money to buy my lovely monster.

'I'm *elated*,' he exploded as we turned into the next street. 'I'm proud of ya, boy.'

We raced round the final corner to help the men install the piano in its new environment, The

B&W. That done, I took the guys out for beer and breakfast... Smiles and laughter all round. As they disappeared into the air, I knew they would be there for my next move. God bless 'em.

'Anyone seen a Steinway go by?' shouted Peter, my former partner.

A lone man, quietly painting the exterior of an Irish bar in a nearby street answered wisely: 'No. What's up, Doc?'

'You must have seen it. You can't miss a thing like that.'

'I'm telling you I didn't see it.'

Peter continued to fume, while the man went on painting.

Within a couple of days I was paid a visit – not by Peter, but by a distraught piano player who naturally wanted to know why there was no piano for him to play on, as a means of earning his living.

'I wanna know what's goin' on,' he stormed, swaggering up to me in The B&W.

'You want to know? That's my piano.' I pointed to the now famous Steinway Grand.

'*Your* piano?' he shouted disbelievingly.

'Well, I'm sorry, David.'

'*You're* sorry?' he shouted back rudely. Poor man. He had been duped. But I was hardly prepared at that point to go into details about the dealings and motives of Peter and his wife. I had a right to earn a living on my own piano.

A few days later, after a very pleasant gig at The B&W, I felt it time to stroll down The High Street and turn the corner into my own street for a reasonably early night. But before I'd reached the front door, I abruptly stopped in horror and disgust as I spotted a dead cat, strung upside down, still bleeding outside my front window. It appeared to have been killed barely an hour before I'd seen it. Turning to my front door, I found both key-holes solidly stuffed with wood so as to make it impossible to insert a key. A mean and wicked mind had been at work.

Leaving the cat there, I rushed along the street and then up The High Street, back to The B&W. 'Oh God,' said John, the proprietor. 'Those awful people. Keep calm, Tony. I'll get a big bag. We'll go and fetch the cat, and then inform Jan.' Jan managed the twin 'local' to The B&W, and was considered pretty smart in dealing with problems between expats in a foreign land…

It was agreed by most of my friends that witchcraft had been at work. It all pointed to the place whence the Steinway had been retrieved. But I was called the biggest thief in Nirvana by one member of that strange family.

'How can I steal my own property? Do you know anything about the law?' I bit back.

Thus it continued. Nasty, petty stuff. Then the notice-boards outside The B&W were vandalized, and finally a poster appeared in front of The Piano Bar, informing everyone that this was the only bar in Nirvana to have had its grand piano stolen... No wonder the Spanish enjoy watching the silly antics of The North Europeans.

CHAPTER 26

Meanwhile, my gig in The B&W was going great guns. Whilst fully aware I was being used to help sell the business for the owners of the leasehold, at least I had a job in which I could relax and show off whatever talents I had been given as a pianist and entertainer. John, who ran the bar, was also a bit of a character, and we soon developed a good double act between us.

Then along came a man and his wife from the UK who, unfortunately for me, did not quite see the venue as a piano bar – despite the fact it was already a business success. They bought the lease on the bar, ousted me, and spent another fortune making the place look like a very expensive lavatory. Some people I know would always approve of this sort of arrangement. But Nirvana is hardly geared up to such cottage tastes, even on a grand scale.

It took a considerable time for the premises to take off again in its new format, by which time the new owners of the lease had well and truly been fleeced by the local authorities and entrepreneurs, ever happy to see foreigners innocently waste their money. It was not long, inevitably, before yet another deflated couple were seen to cross the water, back to dear old England to face whatever music was in store for them, or simply to pick up whatever pieces they could retrieve.

Perhaps this particular couple had at least derived a certain amount of pleasure in seeing the back of Tony Sharp and his Steinway, together with his merry band of removers. The fact is, they had given us little time to move the huge, half-ton instrument. And I clearly recall an incident reflecting their frustration, seeing me play in another bar packed with people whilst The B&W remained empty... I had just got into my stride on an old upright piano in the Bar El Bodegon. Ken, the Dutch owner of the business was digging into the number beside me on his string bass, when up came this angry-looking woman from nowhere who proceeded to fling a grubby piece of paper on to the keys.

'Ignorant bitch,' I growled, dramatically brushing the paper away and on to the floor, and continuing with my improvisation. The applause of approval from the crowded bar carried Ken and me along on the crest of a wave.

At the end of the number, I glanced at the paper I'd picked up from the floor. 'You have until

Wednesday to remove your piano from The B&W – signed (in anger)...

My God. More petty stuff. Could this be for real?

When Wednesday arrived, my men and I were hustled by stony faces to remove the piano as quickly as was well nigh impossible. I was to be punished yet again for someone else's mistakes.

In our haste, we could not remove the pedal mechanism. The bloody thing had jammed, and all of us had forgotten the correct removal sequence. Stupidly I agreed to allow the piano to be loaded on to the waiting truck in its upright position. I would pay heavily for the repairs to that mechanism.

But when the doors were finally banged shut on us, I decided we should all have some fun out of the tragedy. We jumped on to the truck, and I opened the piano lid for a good round of 'Rule Britannia'. As the truck moved along down the street, I proceeded with a stirring chorus of 'Land of Hope & Glory'. Pepe Mesa's chef, Antonio, was a great fan of mine, and he and I enjoyed rounding off the entertainment with our 'singing' and Nazi salutes in full view of the good people of Nirvana. Great cheers erupted on our arrival at the next venue, Maxims, which was situated right next door to The Piano Bar. Since the latter had been taken over with a change of name, the new 'owner' felt he could afford a timely remark as he watched my massive piano being unloaded yet again. 'It's getting *uncomfortably* close, Tony.' Despite all that had transpired, I think he held a sneaking admiration for me.

So my Steinway had a new home. For how long, you may ask? Well, yes... This instrument was fast becoming the most travelled piano in Nirvana. But, bless her, she survived it all.

As she sat there in her new setting, she beckoned me to let rip on her... Booked to perform my sets between the drag shows, I would do just that. But the acts were not any old drag shows. Paul Jurgens, or 'Sapphire' by which name he was known, produced a totally professional act, and women were wont to drag (excuse the pun) their reluctant husbands into the club to see the magnificent legs, if nothing else, of 'Sapphire'. Women were simply envious. And once they had had a few drinks inside them, the men put aside their prejudices, and went along with the laugh.

To balance the smooth sophistication of Sapphire's act, one could always rely on 'Fluff' to do his stuff. A very funny man.

Of course, one day saw the inevitable. My gig collapsed, together with the whole club. Sapphire had his problems (who doesn't?), and a sweet little note was placed on the lid of my Steinway. The piano was due to move again. Luckily, a week before the closure, I had been invited to put my piano into 'Caesar's', an elegant bar in the German quarter of town. 'It's all set up for a piano bar, Tony.' Sandy Schindler, bless him, had come to my rescue.

Once again, I called upon my trusty men to help out bloody Tony Sharp and his piano. But the move, for a pleasant change, turned out to be considerably less frenetic than the two previous occasions. The freehold owner of Maxims, a laid-back Spaniard of the old school, had been informed quite correctly and honourably by Sapphire that the piano was my property and would be removed in a civilized manner.

On the truck once more sat my Steinway, but with her legs off and on her side, her body taking a well-earned rest for a while. Arriving at Caesar's, the men made ready to unload her and carry her gently up the steps and into the bar.

As soon as she was installed and set up, I played a suitable number to a delighted group of well-wishers: the owner and his lady, friends and onlookers… More beer for the men. On Sandy this time. Surely not on Sandy? Are you reading this, my friend?

Sandy Schindler had asked his longstanding friend Barry Gottlieb to run the place. And despite having to release a few peseta notes to me every evening, this man soon became a good friend of mine, both on and off the gig. Barry would remain mad about jazz. My own repertoire stretched right across the board of classical, jazz, ballads and pop, but unfailingly performed with a Sharp twist. I trust I played enough jazz numbers in the course of the evening to make each night bearable for him.

Barry's intelligence and sensitivity on all issues and aspects of life appealed to me, and though his interpretation of Tony Bennett numbers raised more than a few eyebrows when he opened his lungs, I enjoyed my gig immensely. The Steinway looked and sounded fabulous in the cool, spacious room. Yet too many 'Ee-ups' from the north of England were loath to loosen the old purse-strings…

'Ey, 'e's bloody good on that piano, i'n't 'e?'

'Well, buy 'im a drink, then,' said Barry who needed to earn a living, too.

But the purse-strings would all too often be kept closed. And within a year and a half, the gig folded.

No notice, of course. But as I say, musicians are used to this treatment. Thank God some of us get a kick out of living on the edge.

But as luck would have it, a bright Spanish businessman had approached me a few days before the closure of Caesar's, and asked me to go and see him at his new bar. He wanted ME AND MY STEINWAY... Was The Almighty taking care of me, after all? Surely not Tony Sharp?

Off came the legs of my big baby again. Her body lay down on the floor of the truck, and up the road she went once more. No chorus this time, no Rule Britannia, no Besame Mucho. Just a few knowing nods and winks from expats who'd seen it all before. Where's it off to, this time? Does an old Steinway have to suffer this indignity for ever?

Safely installed in another new home called 'Madison's', a huge bunch of flowers was placed beside the piano by the Spanish proprietor's wife. Surely the funeral of my lovely Steinway will not take place here? In front of all these people? Have they no faith?

More beers and laughs. A photo-call for the proprietor and my men and good wishes all round. I had a new gig.

Would the circus never end? Would Tony Sharp wake up to the realities of life? For too long he had drifted in the sea of uncertainty in which so many musicians appear to thrive. Back in London, excellent pros would turn down attractive gigs abroad for fear of losing the chance of grabbing a hot, fragile seat in a top musical or even a recording session. There was always something, they believed, waiting for them round the corner.

I have long understood the lure of London. Having lived in the West End for twenty odd years, I'd be a liar to say I don't miss it.

But the grass is always greener on the other side. In London, I rarely enjoyed good cheap booze or an abundance of warm sunshine. Nor did I have a Steinway grand on which to indulge myself. Yet even this pleasure would have its price, and its use wickedly restricted.

In Madison's, my new boss José Miguel set to work on his customers. He was a fine host, and for the most part he enjoyed giving me my head on the piano. He even joined me in energetic interpretations of 'Granada', dancing in high camp, tongue-in-cheek bravado. He was a gentleman in his behaviour towards me, and the venture proved a great success.

Then came the forebodings of trouble. The woman upstairs, just one in a block of apartments, complained about the piano. Would I learn from this experience, or would I ignore the warning and allow circumstances to drown me when I opened my own bar?

On several occasions the police were called. Yet José Miguel would always manage to mollify them, and the music would resume. After all, he was a Spaniard.

But one night, his son, Sammi, asked me to play my own version of 'Take Five'. It was early, and there was no one in the bar except Sammi and me. As I began to let go in the improvisation, allowing those marvellously rich harmonics and special growl in the bass register of the Steinway full rein, suddenly, from nowhere it seemed, José Miguel came rushing into the place in a mad temper. 'For God's sake, don't play like that,' he screamed... What had got into him? He'd heard me play the number on several occasions, and had always approved. He dashed up to the bar and got on with his work, whilst I proceeded to 'cool' it.

At the end of the evening, over a good long drink, José Miguel apologized for his outburst. 'It's that *bloody* woman,' he said bitterly. 'She has nothing better to do than complain.' It would be little over a year, when those words and sentiments would find more than an echo in my own place.

CHAPTER 27

In the Spring of 1996, a short but polite letter from my neighbours back in London arrived under my door. Would I be interested in 'key money' for my flat there?

For more than ten years, they had expressed an interest in my tiny pied-à-terre, with the idea of extending their property from the ground floor, upwards. And for more than ten years, I had firmly but politely turned down the ongoing offer, not least for the fact that I found it the best 'humping' pad I'd ever had... Considering the vast amount of sexual activity I enjoyed in my 'single' bed there, it was simply incredible I never broke it. The same could not be said of my future comfortable double sofa-bed in Nirvana which I would break twice during a prolonged fallow period in my love-life. Mustn't grumble, mustn't grumble. Life is full of irony, and the dishes cannot always be the ones we imagine we have ordered.

But my neighbours in London persisted. Moreover, the situation and circumstances had changed. Here I was, resident in Nirvana, moving from bar to bar with my bloody great piano and little prospect of a permanent, reliable source of income. I was running out of music bars.

The offer from London had miraculously doubled from the original sum, and I saw at once that this was my opportunity to clinch a deal. I would go to London and discuss the idea of buying my pied-à-terre (rented from The Church Commissioners), and then selling it directly to my neighbours. With the cash difference I could build a piano bar in my Spanish house. A trifle more than 'key money' would be necessary to do this, but if the cash covered the cost, I would be satisfied.

A deal was struck, and once lawyers' fees had been paid, we could all show a smile. That we did. And the money left over was just enough to make my dream come true. Little did I know what I was facing. For I was intent upon the project. It seemed such a civilized way of earning a living: playing the Steinway and entertaining in my own house with just sufficient money to put food in my mouth and enjoy a social drink or two. Surely, no reasonable human being could object to this, particularly as I would religiously stop playing every evening at 12 midnight, and the neighbours each side of me were here for a maximum of two months of the year in the height of the summer? Surely noisy tourists letting off steam into the small hours in the street, raucous motor-bikes, Spanish just being Spanish, and screaming English girls in the sea, expressing that special alchemy of fear, elation and sexual stimulation – ravished in their trance if not always in reality; surely all these ingredients of life in a sea-side town would supersede a mean concern for a Steinway piano, and one, moreover, played with some skill and feeling? But I had underestimated the extent to which the conspiracies of my neighbour would reach. The fact is, of all the bitches allowed to roam and do their worst in Nirvana, my neighbour takes the biscuit.

Bereft of the grace and elegance of certain noble animal breeds, this one in human form strode through life with the panache of Heinrich Himmler in drag. Come to think of it, in physical appearance she bore a remarkable resemblance to that infamous director of genocide – on a good day.

I am not without compassion. For indeed, others have spoken of her as a pariah that should have been strangled at birth. And to be honest, I would much prefer Adolf Hitler to have been my neighbour. At least he appreciated piano players, having lived with one in his 'student' days. He might even have turned a blind eye to my 'half-Jewish' blood and the credentials of my piano if I had convinced him Wagner had expressed glowing enthusiasm for the qualities of a Steinway.

But to The Bitch, the beauties of a Steinway would mean nothing. I would soon suffer the consequences of her wicked ways. So in blissful ignorance, silly old Tony Sharp forged ahead. With two months' notice given to José Miguel (no one's ever been that considerate to me) and a final move of the Steinway agreed to by the men, we ploughed on to build the bar.

Why should I reproach myself? The result looked simply stunning, and I congratulated my builder and the men on a job executed with all those artistic touches which come so easily to the Spanish. It's in the blood. Surely my neighbour would be won over when she saw it? Surely she would see an opportunity for her two sons to have free piano lessons? But no. She brusquely refused an invitation to my opening night...

'Come and have a drink with me, Helga,' I called to her in all innocence, the day before the big event.

'I haven't got time for that,' she replied rudely.

On opening night I discovered the reason for her rudeness. A letter from her solicitor here in Nirvana was delivered by hand to me in the bar. It requested I should call on him to discuss Helga's disapproval of my 'new' terrace. This in fact had basically been straightened up by my builders, tiled and beautified with a pretty balustrade, resulting in my customers being able, in her words "to study a way into my house, and rob me." How pathetic. But this was merely the hors d'oeuvre to her real gripe. 'Denuncias' would follow, producing *four* closures and the eventual prohibition of the use of my piano during opening hours. For ten months of the year, while my customers were denied the pleasure of some live piano music, she would strut around the nerve centre of her own country, directing the course of my business, here in Nirvana. In my frustration and not a little anger I wrote, in good Spanish, to The Mayor...

One day, maybe, there will be some justice meted out to those of us who struggle to earn a meagre living in the south of Spain. With EC funds for motorways and such already spent, Andalucia, it appears, has little to do with a new, 'clean' Europe. Good old-fashioned corruption prevails. It's in the blood. That's the way it is. Who will change it? The EC? If it's impossible to fight corruption and it is deemed impolite even to mention the word, what chance have civil rights?

I put the curt letter aside, and determined we should all have a good time. My Spanish bar-boy, Raul, got stuck into his work with youthful vigour and charm, and I was soon on that piano, producing some sounds to stir the blood and effect a fair consumption of alcohol. The takings were very good, and I paid Raul his money, as I would every subsequent night. With his substantial tips, he went to his favourite disco as happy as a sandboy. Trouble would soon come my way, but I concentrated on making the bar a success. A day at a time.

Day 3 proved particularly appealing to us all. My little cat, Tabsy (she has a special chapter in this book) decided she, too, would like to play the piano. It brought the house down. It's all in my diary 1997, July 3rd: Tabsy plays piano. I have witnesses to the event.

Hot on the heels of this pleasant evening came the first closure of the bar. It transpired to be an especially dramatic affair. For in my absence, the bar, which was also my house, had been taped up by The EXCMO. AYUNTAMIENTO – short for The Very Excellent Town Hall, a description which never fails to bring a cynical smile even to the proudest of the proud Spanish. As I returned from a meal in a local restaurant, I spotted the tape, sealing and barring entrance to the house. My blood rose quickly to the boil, and in rampant anger I stripped off the tape, and telephoned my closest confidant. Together we went to see the Chief of Police.

'Oh, we were told he doesn't live there.'

'Well, he *does*,' said my friend in correct Spanish. 'He has nowhere else to go. It's his house.'

A new report was produced on the spot, and back we went to the house to discuss the next move.

Endless visits to The Town Hall followed, a slap on the wrist and a fine for stripping off their precious tape, more money handed over for bits of paper, more visits from the police to test which way I'd jump. And all the while I knew The Bitch was pulling the strings. One man in The Town Hall looked me straight in the eye with an understanding expression: 'Tony. Ella tiene *mucho* dinero,' adding 'she will never give up.' Was he trying to tell me something I didn't already know?

As the months passed by, I received a letter from The Town Hall which at first sight appeared very good news indeed. At a special meeting of the councillors, it said, "WE FIND IN YOUR FAVOUR."

I called my builder, and we raised our glasses in premature celebration in my bar. 'Congratulations,' he said expansively, after reading the letter. 'You have your licence.'

''You sure?' My scepticism could not be obliterated that easily. And there were still 'a' and 'b' clauses on the paper to be dealt with…

I phoned my 'Projecto' man who then prepared the necessary documents.

When he turned up with the papers completed, I paid him the required 69,000 pesetas, and we celebrated with another drink. As one does.

'Now, Antonio,' I said with a sigh, 'what else do I have to do to get this licence?'

'That's it, Tony. You've done everything necessary. Tranquilo.'

Tranquilo. Their favourite word. You are supposed to remain calm while someone thinks of something else for you to pay for, and something else, and so on... until you tear your hair out, or it falls out in protest.

Three days later I have a visit from the bully policeman, holding papers in his hot, angry hand. No licence, of course, but a demand I should spend more money. 'Have you a limitador?' he asks.

'No, amigo. What's a limitador?'

'Oh, you have to have a limitador.'... Well, it cost me 224,000 pesetas, so as to enable them to read what decibels my bar issued every second or fraction of a second, regardless of any sound reaching the houses either side of me through my thick walls.

Okay. I swallow that begrudgingly at the time. But where is the licence? No licence, of course. Then they close me because I *haven't* the licence. SECOND CLOSURE.

I then employ a lawyer outside the town with a different viewpoint. More expense. The Town Hall is "no correcto," says the lawyer. She's right. If they had been 'correcto', I would *not* have had to employ a lawyer... You fancy a piano bar in Spain?

After two and a half months' closure, my lawyer succeeded in extracting my licence from The Town Hall. So, considerably poorer, but 'armed' with the assurance they would never close me again ('They will just warn you,' she said, 'if it is necessary to reduce noise,') I proceeded to set to work again and enjoy my bar.

The THIRD CLOSURE took place on the basis of false readings and a police report which clearly stated it was impossible to measure the decibels in the street adjoining my bar – because 'the street was too noisy and too narrow'.

You *still* fancy a piano bar in Spain?

While struggling to earn a living without the use of the piano, a Spanish lady friend turned the scales for me by persuading the councillor responsible for my case to allow me the use of the piano again, but with the 'top down'. Now, there's no doubt about it: a Steinway full concert grand, even an antique like mine, punches out some decibels - beautiful, stirring sounds, enough to shift any remaining ants from the pants or knickers of the most stubborn among us. With the piano lid down, it can still do this, yet perhaps the decibels issuing from the instrument are sufficiently reduced to satisfy an arbitrary 'law'. A piano player worth his salt, therefore, can always compensate, and defy the uninitiated.

The councillor phoned the Chief of Police from his Town Hall Office. 'Tony's playing tonight. Okay?'

With kisses for my lady friend and a firm handshake for the councillor, I set to work once more to entertain the public. With the piano top down, I played on – up to 12 midnight, and fooled about behind the bar as usual. But within a week, The Bitch had left Nirvana in a rage, and returned to her own land, determined to 'nail' Sharp for good. Her lawyer here had clear instructions...

Before long, I received a letter with unequivocal orders from The Town Hall: I must instruct an independent technical firm to test my walls for levels of sound extraction: i.e. they must extract a minimum of 75 decibels. This, of course, and all subsequent reparations had to be achieved at my own expense. In the meantime, I was informed the limitador would be a thing of the past - 224,000 pesetas (twelve hundred pounds or so Sterling) up in smoke. Happy days.

To cut a long story short, my walls were found to extract 68 decibels: bloody good for a private house, of course, and more than the 65 requirement of my licence. But The Town Hall had dragged a 1994 law out of a draw, doubtless on the instructions of my absentee neighbour. Did I want Hitler's bunker, just so that I could play to the public again? You *still* fancy a piano bar in Spain?

Yes, Himmler in Drag remained determined. She would destroy that Tony Sharp who had jilted her, knocked down her hideous wall, and then opened a piano bar next door. Three times Mr Sharp turned down 'offers' from her to buy his house. But Mr Sharp had a pretty good idea of the value of his property. He wasn't *that* silly.

CHAPTER 28

I ploughed on. But it was only a matter of time before the FOURTH CLOSURE. The Town Hall soon realized I had no intention of chopping my bar about in order to produce that arbitrary sound extraction. Besides, it remained my house. So I continued playing till the inevitable visit.

As expected, the police turned up while my neighbour sat ensconced in her bunker, a thousand or more miles away. The Town Hall sent *four* policemen to deliver a tiny piece of paper, summoning me to the presence, next day.

'But my neighbour's not here,' I pleaded with the senior police officer. 'You can see my bar is full of people, enjoying the music. Can she hear it a thousand miles away? Am I *that* noisy?'

The policeman looked slightly embarrassed, but said I had to close. Just like that. My customers could not believe the stupidity of it all – the injustice, the lack of finesse, the fact they had sent *four* policemen to deliver that puny piece of paper. What an insult to one's intelligence.

A few days later, a kindly Spanish restaurateur in my street spoke up on my behalf... 'Look, Tony's been here a long time. And he's a good man. His bar is his only income. Let him run it just as a bar.'

So, for me the great compromise meant the dream of my own piano bar had come to an end. I would run it as an alcoholics' bar and leave it at that.

Finally they left me alone. The Town Hall was happy, whilst The Bitch still tried to stir things via her solicitor – until I employed another Spanish lawyer who worked for a powerful firm in London. Those impressive and beautifully constructed letters finally got 'Himmler' off my back. No one would stop me playing in my own house outside working hours.

Of course, it wasn't *all* anger and frustration, constant arguments with my neighbour, meetings with the authorities, closures, borrowing money on compound interest, tying a noose round my own neck... Having taken to drink at an early age, like a decent duck to water, I would enjoy a distinct advantage in my eventual job as barman in my own establishment. Discussions over the counter tended to be initiated by me in an attempt to get folks to imbibe, and make my own life more bearable. The strategy worked, and before the evening drew to a close, people of the most unlikely connections under normal circumstances were buying me and each other drinks, and laughing and joking as though we'd been buddies for years. All good fun, and a little business for yours truly.

But as every bar owner knows, customers can be divided into three main categories: a pleasure to serve, utter bores, or plain darned nuisances. If one is lucky enough to get rid of the last mentioned category, one is left with a difficult balancing act. For sadly, too many bores have money. And every bar owner has to take money. He is not in the game for his health, despite the opportunity to crack and share in a few jokes and partake in that glass or two, or three or more... I am told I have the sort of personality that draws customers to me. Unfortunately, it draws all three categories so far mentioned. If only one could choose. But life is not like that.

I have some wonderful times imprinted upon my memory, and some bad ones, too. And people are people. Besides, I am still sufficiently compos mentis to distinguish certain characteristics between them - in face of the insidious fashion for lumping everyone together. When I'm in my box I might be the same as the next man, not before.

And in order to forestall that inevitable event until the proper time, I decided to sell the house and move to a place where I could live in peace. Yet I keep meeting folks who never cease to remind me of those dramatic days in Nirvana, and my bar in particular. Some of those good people, I'm happy to say, have become close friends; others, well...

My best customers, by far, were The Irish: darned good spenders, very charming, funny, generous and outgoing. I loved 'em, and still do. Not only was I able to earn a wee living with them as customers, but also have a fun time in the process...

The English (my own lot, one could argue), torn between seemingly irreconcilable poles of identity, find themselves emasculated and thrown into a heavily guarded corner of political correctness, while thieves with preferential treatment under a daft, twisted law rob their homes, and international terrorists organize their vile business from English soil. (Any chance of the situation changing before publication of this book?) The English, understandably, are not much of a laugh these days. There are exceptions, thank Goodness, for, discouraged at home, they come to Spain to allow the remnants of traditional humour free rein. The sun is a special bonus.

The Germans. Well, what can one say? Careful, Sharp. But as my Dutch friend 'Peter the Pest' aptly put it one night in my bar, "the thinnest book in the world just has to be 'A Thousand Years of German Humour'." It's *not enough*, I say. With the best will in the world, I don't believe the Germans will ever catch on to the subtleties of

English, Irish or Jewish humour. It's hard enough for an American gentile to fathom. Sometimes harder... And yet the best Germans who visit Nirvana, particularly among the professional classes, could give some of us English a lesson or two in refined behaviour. But there are always exceptions, are there not?

In my bar, one could see everything: a true microcosm of the larger world. It was an international venue, and I was usually very happy to see the Spanish enter and join in the fun with us expats. After all, I am, I suppose, still a resident alien. Who cares? And I cared not who entered my bar, as long as he or she behaved. Indeed, I commend the Spanish on their manners, but like any other nationals, well, there's always one, isn't there? The man I have in mind was a nuisance whom I tolerated for far too long. Since he's a self-confessed anarchist, I have no hesitation in mentioning his name: Eduardo, the beggar... After scrounging in the precincts of the Parish Church, he would trot along to my bar, and proceed to nudge and goad my customers into buying him a drink. 'SPAIN is *DIRRERENT*,' he'd shout, over and over again. My tolerance level eventually blew a fuse, and I refused to serve him unless he put down his money first. I much prefer the humane, civilized Spanish tradition of 'paying at the end'. But with this man, whom I befriended and stupidly bought a few drinks in return for a few Spanish words and respect for the host country, it seemed impossible to strike a balance. He hated the English with a passion, and anyone (except the Spanish) with money. Yet he would accept drinks from a capitalist until the cows came home. Do they come home, in Spain?

One night, Eduardo decided he'd create a disturbance in my bar. I was already on the piano, striking out a soulful number to a packed audience. Eduardo determined he would vocalize the rhythmic pattern I had set, in the most irritating way. He knew what he was doing. He then began to shout and stare me out.

Blast the man. I got off the piano and phoned the police. Wrong decision, for it would just be my luck to get the worst kind of policeman, another racist and a known bully. If only they had sent 00-11 who played my piano louder than I, and grinned away happily with his gun in his holster as he bashed out some form of Flamenco. With another slurp of my Lagavulin whisky, he would continue. A close friend of a Spanish bass guitarist who became the sole supplier of limitadors for the bars of Nirvana, he'd have made a good front man for a police band – *without* a limitador. But they sent 00... No, the bully would never have the sophistication of 00-7. I believe he's moved on now, but he used to do the rough stuff for The Town Hall. Loathed by many a bar owner and by fellow police alike, he strode through Nirvana with The Town Hall's blessing. I wonder why?

Anyway, he turned up at my place with his posse of underling admirers, waiting on his orders. Well-known for his love of closing British-run bars, this man simply talked to Eduardo and instructed me in the procedure for a petition of complaint from my customers. A waste of time. And Eduardo knew it. When the police had gone, he puffed with pride, and began his despicable act all over again. I could hardly believe it. But as soon as I uttered my rarely used F-word from the piano, my tougher customers rose from their seats, and hustled Eduardo out of the door. I myself was not supposed to touch him. Enough said. The evening was ruined. It's not impossible the man has gone to work for whatever anarchic cause is available to him. A quick end would be merciful. He'd be lucky.

I am absolutely certain Peter the Pest would love to see himself mentioned in a book, despite a somewhat derogatory description attached to his name. Dutch by birth and nature, Peter or Pieter is a free thinker and tolerant of most things.

I, too, prided myself on my tolerance level until I met this man. He seemed to have lots of money, and a willingness to spend quite a bit of it on drinks in my bar. The downside to this pattern was his insistence upon being over-friendly with my customers. You know the type: the loner with cash who can't resist touching-up folk and boring them to death.

I knew Peter was a decent fellow by nature, so I took him aside one day, bought him a drink and made him promise to stay away until his 'Princess' turned up; the 'Princess' being none other than his wife for the last thirty-five years. Sounds romantic, doesn't it? Until you have the 'Princess' thrust down your throat every night.

'I can't *wait* for your 'Princess' to arrive.' I couldn't resist. A few customers sniggered, but Peter took it on the chin. He agreed to my suggestion as good as gold. When at last the 'Princess' arrived, I don't know why, but I felt somewhat sorry for him. I think I bought him another drink in sympathy. Needless to say, the divorce went through, and within a few weeks he had found himself a new Princess upon whom he would spend a small fortune. And once again, my customers and I were bored out of our brains.

Moreover, one night Peter brought in a German couple, and proceeded to bemoan the loss of his new Princess (it doesn't take long to lose a Princess). After a while, the Germans paid their bill together with that of Peter, and left. He then turned to two German ladies whom I'd known for some years, nice quiet ladies from Hamburg…

'Peter,' one said, not unkindly, 'we've heard your story many times before. I'm afraid we can't help you with your problem.' These ladies, likewise, paid their bill and departed. How on earth can one bore *four* Germans? Peter could.

But this was not enough for him. He then tried his chances with four new customers who'd just arrived from London, in need of a few relaxed, uncomplicated drinks and a chat with the landlord. 'That's it, Peter,' I said smartly. 'I want you to leave, my friend. You're emptying the bar for me, and I can't afford it.'

He looked at me with hurt surprise. But he had to go. I have seen him many times since writing this, and I trust there are no hard feelings. But only he can resolve his problems. I have my own.

One summer, I was paid a visit by a mad Icelandic singer. A woman of immense structure, "a bit on the lines of The Albert Hall", as P.G. Wodehouse would have described her, she was drawn irresistibly to my Steinway grand. She had followed me around the town from bar to bar until I ceased to see her, and had forgotten all about her with her 'singing' and most unnerving stare.

But she had discovered Sharp's new music venue, and hoped she had found her niche. The place was packed that night. My barboy Raul was working full out, and a great buzz filled the air. I can't remember the number I was playing at the time, but it certainly wasn't anything to do with the song which Iceland now proceeded to exude to a startled audience. Now, I have always possessed a perverse sense of humour, and the lady, in any case, was rude enough to burst into her own song uninvited - over the top of a completely different piece already in progress at the hands of yours truly. So why should I stop playing? No, I thought, let's have some fun. The result was beautifully excruciating and great entertainment. Moreover, Iceland leant back on the piano which moved with the weight. How can one woman move a half-ton piano on her own? She could, and what is more, opened her lungs further. With the whole performance over, she announced in raptured tones: 'Oh, I *love* this place. I shall come here every night.'

'Must you?' I responded in my best English. 'Perhaps every *other* night?'

The customers loved it. My cruel remark seemed to go over her head. But then, perhaps it wasn't so cruel, after all. For no sooner had I left the piano to join Raul behind the bar than he informed me her two Danish guests who still sat on the terrace overlooking the beach had not bought a drink the whole evening…

'No correcto, Tony,' he stated succinctly.

'Okay, Raul. Don't worry. I'll handle it…'

'Oh, no thank you,' they said when I politely asked if they would like a drink. 'We have to be up early tomorrow at 9.a.m. – to catch a plane to Copenhagen.'

Just as I was about to 'lock them out' and turn out the lights over my terrace in disgust and some anger, they changed their minds. 'Perhaps we will have two small beers.'

CHAPTER 29

The next night, four terribly English people descended on me, and took up their positions on my comfortable, half-circle leather sofa near the piano.

'Good evening. What would you like to drink?' I enquired as usual.

'Do we have to? We've heard you're a very good pianist.'

'Well, that's nice to know. But I still have to make a living, I'm afraid.'

'Oh dear,' one responded disappointedly. 'In that case, I'll have a water.' My face stayed the same, but I groaned within.

'I'll have a Sprite,' said another. The man followed up with 'And a small beer for me.'

The last customer was even keener. 'I'm afraid I don't drink. Could you play Rachmaninoff's Second Piano Concerto, please?'

'With or without orchestra?' I'd had enough, and concentrated on some newly arrived customers who wanted a good skinful. The 'terribly English' received their beverages eventually, but were soon discouraged. And the bar filled with drinkers and happy people.

Comfortably seated one lunch-time at a table on the terrace of my favourite fish restaurant in Nirvana, I overheard part of a conversation between a quiet American (rare in itself) and his wife. He seemed knowledgeable about a wide range of subjects without appearing pushy, arrogant or selfish in the manner of so many male 'know-alls'. His wife exuded a refined, civilizing femininity, likewise a welcome contrast to the crudities of certain other liberated women who had had occasion to 'grace' my bar.

After a decent interval, I introduced myself and invited them to Sharp's place. They turned up that very evening with another couple – a Spanish lady and her Swedish husband. The bar began to fill with a variety of interesting people, most of whom were not only good drinkers but also endowed with character and some grey matter between the ears. At an appropriate moment, out came my talking parrot. The Winston Churchill oration produced smiles and laughter, as usual, and then I judged it time for the 'Spanish' sketch.

'Don't mention The Armada,' I began sotto voce. 'They don't like it up them.' A few more giggles. Then raising my voice to after-dinner volume: 'Queen Elizabeth told Philip to *bugger off...* in *no uncertain terms.*' More laughter. And it was then that my American friend, a lecturer specializing in Spanish history, decided to quiz his Spanish guest as to whether or not I had been talking through my 'proverbial'. Why should the parrot take all the stick?

'No,' she said. 'He's quite right. We've never forgotten it.'

'But why do you blame the English for the disaster? It was your fault.'

There was no answer to that. The Spanish lady wisely returned to her drink, and my American friend went on to other matters.

'Two more beers, please.'

'Right, sir.'

'Oh, and before you go back on the piano, put another gin in there, will you, Tony, and a Tia Maria for Maggie?'

'Certainly, Fred.'

'You're wasted.'

'Pardon?'

'Don't forget my Bailey's, Tony.'

'All right, Joan. I'll be with you in a jiffy.'

'You're wasted.'

The repeated remark from a tortured-looking woman I'd never seen before, only served to irritate and remind me of all the mistakes and sins of omission back in London, where perhaps I might have made money if I had not been so stubborn or stupid.

Might, of course, is the operative word, for I had known so many good musicians who had been taken to the cleaners by ever-enterprising, dishonourable men. The music business is notorious for rip-offs, and it doesn't need a Roger Cook to remind musicians of this fact. No doubt there is the odd, honest bloke lurking somewhere in a forgotten room along the corridor. Is he dead?

Nevertheless, I still regret turning down contracts as a writer and musician in the course of more than one offer from famous record companies. You have to 'get up there' before you can start calling the tune. Ironic, isn't it? If the public only knew...

'You're wasted.'

Christ Almighty. How many more times would this woman say that? She sat there, intently inebriated, while I returned to the piano. As I played to a packed audience, more than happy to keep quiet and listen, she rabbited on to her man about...

'Right, folks,' I snapped. 'I think we'll have another drink, don't you?' I left the piano, and returned to the bar to serve ever thirsty customers. But I was not to be allowed an easy escape. My tormentor lurched over to the bar and plonked herself on a stool in a position where she could inspect the array of almost empty flasks of washing-up liquid, trying to hide under my sink...

'Disgusting,' I could see forming on her lips. But she returned to the subject in hand. 'We have a pub in London, and...' She proceeded to boast of a string of well-known musicians she employed, and... I had enjoyed working with most of them. But I kept my mouth shut for a change. I saw no point in allowing myself to be drawn. Besides, I still had a bar, full of real drinkers.

'You're wasted,' she droned on. 'Fancy ending up in this bloody backwater.'

It's always sad to see a person struggle with a drug problem, particularly when he or she is young.

An English girl visited my bar one evening, still high as a kite – even though she was supposed to be 'drying out'. I had seen a photo of her, as a model. What a beautiful girl she had once been. Now she was taking on the features and lines of a frustrated spinster. My God, what a swift, terrible change.

The boyfriend, a young Spanish lad, put in charge of her medication, remained calm and very polite. 'If you want me to take her out, just say.'

It was good to know there would be no problems if she got out of hand. So I relaxed, served a few customers, and walked over to my piano. No sooner had I started to play than the girl screamed out – was it in ecstasy or pain? Or some kind of delicious agony? She had a smile on her face, but her eyes remained dilated, focusing nowhere in particular.

At this point, as more customers entered the bar, I thought it prudent to ask the lad to take her out. Miraculously, they both slipped away quietly, and I got on serving my drinkers.

Fifteen minutes later, the couple returned, and the girl made for the Ladies, and locked herself in. I didn't think much about it until I heard running water. She was having a shower… Most of my female customers realize it's a shower for my personal use when the bar is closed to the public. But the girl lived on another planet. As she continued to abandon herself to limitless water, I knocked politely on the door. Amazingly, she undid the lock, and poked her head out. With the bathroom in a complete mess, bottles of disinfectant all over the place, and the floor flooded, she 'hid', naked, behind a tiny hand-towel with a curious expression on her face… 'Do I owe you anything?' she said, innocently.

It's just a thought, but maybe my place should have been re-named The M.D. Bar – for the Mentally Disturbed. Perhaps a grant from the EC would have been possible, if I had guaranteed a sufficient number of nutters. It wouldn't have been difficult – in Nirvana. And there again, even my neighbour might have been persuaded to join us, encouraged by the men in white coats; constrained in a straight-jacket and force-fed a dose of Sharp at full pelt on his Steinway. She'd then appreciate the thick wall between her house and mine, and drop all her complaints. Some hope. She was not made that way.

CHAPTER 30

Back in '92, when I returned to Nirvana to take up permanent residence, I had no idea of the drama that would ensue as a result of gutting my Fisherman's cottage a few years later and turning it into the elegant piano bar it became. I was happy enough to potter about, picking up the odd job, playing other people's pianos, organs, whatever one liked to call them. Besides, when I'd arrived at the house, put down my bags, looked across over the sea, and then ran up the stone steps to the terrace I set eyes upon my favourite animal: the cat. But in this instance, it was four cats – mummy and her three babies, each a different colour to mummy and very, very sweet.

Eventually, the babies would become my house cats, and mummy would go and leave me to it. Herbie, the black and white male, was the first to trot down from the terrace and on to the patio and into the house. He was the one with the personality and would lead the chorus of hungry mouths when my time came to take over mummy's role.

The other male cat I called Isabel, since 'she' possessed wonderful Spanish eyes of stunning beauty. Some time later, I quickly renamed him José when I spotted his great big bollocks as he lay a foot away from me at the end of the patio, one fine afternoon...

'Oh, I'm so sorry, Isabel. I thought you were a girl. I'll call you José, now. How about that? José's a nice name.'

I always talk to cats like this, silly old arse, Tony.

The other cat of the trio was Blackie, a beautiful girl who, one day, I would sadly lose. I looked all over the town for her, put an ad in the window of CAS – Costa Animal Society, etc, but no Blackie. I'd had her spayed, and a lady friend of mine nursed her back to health before returning her to me. She seemed very happy to be home, and I watched her joyously playing with her brothers without a care in the world, or even a mention of hysterectomies or arguments with outsiders.

But she had gone when I returned from a short trip to England. The young lady who willingly took on the job of looking after the cats felt very guilty about Blackie's disappearance, but I assured her I laid no blame on her whatsoever: these things happen.

It's sad, but that's life.

Of the three siblings, Herbie, undoubtedly, was the one with the outstanding character. I brought him up as a gentleman. Perhaps I should not have interfered. Yet it may well have been his nature, for he would stand back at meal times, to allow any female first choice of the food. Many's the time I would have to open another tin, so Herbie would not starve.

But of course, when it came to freshly roasted chicken, Herbie was the first to appear on the scene – all keen and anxious to get his share. As for liver, he'd go wild with desire... One fine day, I came home from shopping, and in need of a good stiff whisky before feeding the tribe. I'd bought some fresh liver – no, not calf's liver, I hasten to add, but pig's liver: here in Spain, it's not as pungent as the offal in England, but if it's fresh, it's soft and pleasant to the taste, and very cheap. As I nosed and sipped a wee Lagavulin dram with customary contentment, a tiny mouse trotted into the room from my patio – on his way home to his parents who, I discovered later, lived under my cooker (at least until more suitable accommodation could be found)... 'Oh, look at that, Herbie,' I said as Herbie stood in front of me, waiting for his liver. Herbie had ample time to catch the mouse and do his stuff with it, but he knew what was best for him: he'd leave the mousing lark to the others, if they chose to waste their time and energy in this senseless pursuit. *He'd* go for the liver, every time. With a casual movement of his paw, he brushed the mouse aside with aristocratic indifference, and looked up to me with those expressive, knowing eyes of his. 'You were saying, Tony? Time for the liver?' A wonderful, priceless moment I will never forget.

It was Herbie who'd trot up the street with Blackie, his sister, to meet me coming down in the opposite direction, after work at the B&W. They'd trot side by side and be half-way up the street as I turned the corner on my way back from the bar. Now, how on earth did they know I was on my way home?

Herbie outlived his brother and sister, and probably most of the other cats who would come my way as a result of a very productive little black cat I called Sneaky who made my house her home for a considerable time. Perhaps it was Herbie who was the 'responsible' father of quite a number of her many children. Certainly, a black and white youngster I called Snappy could not have been anyone other than Herbie's son. He was so close to his father in looks and temperament, except for his habit of snapping at my fingers when I lent over to feed him a tasty bit of meat.

As time went by, the cats came and went; Sneaky produced litter after litter, and finally she gave birth to three tabbies, one of whom survived to become my little treasure and soul mate. This tiny kitten caught the cat-flu, very early on, and I spotted her clinging to her mother's side, anxious to survive. She had stubby paws which looked totally out of proportion to the rest of her body. What a funny-looking little cat, I thought at the time. But her constant sneezing yet determination to live prompted me to contact the vet immediately.

He arrived in a few minutes, and I held the cat still while he injected her with... Okay, she accepted that with good grace. But then came the second needle...

'Ouch.' She bit us both hard, and ran off to find her mother or just get away from those cruel men who kept sticking needles in her.

Three hours later, I was lying on my bed, having a quiet siesta or perhaps more of a daydream, contemplation, whatever, when the little cat came running into the house, jumped on my bed and immediately snuggled up to me. 'I'm yours,' she said. And that was that. Tabsy was mine. I never saw her mother again. She knew I'd look after her very special daughter.

Herbie stayed on, making good friends with Tabsy. But then, one day, a huge ginger tom up on my terrace began to cause trouble. I suppose all my cats one would term feral. But this ginger monster was no cat of mine. When I went up on to the terrace and got near him, he'd hiss and bite my leg. Moreover, he'd frighten my gentle Herbie who'd do his best to protect himself. But Herbie too often expected *me* to sort out his problems. I decided to have a chat with him. I placed him on the top of my huge Steinway grand, stroked his body with affection, and looked him straight in the eye...

'Herbie, dear. I love you lots and lots. But I can't fight *all* your battles. Life is tough. You have to learn to fight, yourself, darling. You *do* understand, don't you?'

He nudged my face and nodded. The next day, Herbie had gone. Three and a half weeks passed, and I felt anxious and very, very guilty... When he turned up, supported by young Tabsy at his side, he appeared in a dreadful state. One front paw had been badly damaged, his ears were scratched, he was moaning. Oh, God.

The vet patched him up as best he could, pumping him with antibiotics galore, and in time Herbie 'recovered', but remained vitually a three-legged cat in practical terms. I think he held up his bad paw for show and sympathy, since one day, when he'd seen I'd had enough of his 'moaning', he suddenly put his paw firmly down on the tiles and walked along with me as right as rain. 'You *can* do it, Herbie. Good boy.' He seemed pleased with my remark, and puffed with pride.

Oh, I love cats. But Herbie knew that Tabsy would claim my total devotion one day, and of course, he did his best to square things with me. A great cat.

CHAPTER 31

Yes, it was Tabsy who'd be the real love of my life.

She has now 'passed on', but is waiting for me to go with her to the other world. I have seen her ghost and have felt her presence many, many times. And still do.

Back in 2003, while preparing ideas and chapters for another book which remained in manuscript form, she was with me in the bar, watching the progress of my work and waiting for me to 'pen' her special chapter. I had the distinct feeling she knew she had but one more year to live, and that I knew, too.

This is what I wrote at that time – and include in this book in her honour:

She knows. She's just given me that beautiful, knowing look. Today is the day I will put her chapter on the screen. I've had a chat with her, of course, and she knows she will be famous as a result of this book.

Silly old fool, you say? Talking to, and about a cat like that. What do I care? Cat lovers will know what I'm about.

Cats don't ask for much: just food and water, warm shelter and a little love. I am fully aware a number of people are disturbed when I say my cat gives me more peace than almost any human being of my acquaintance. But it's true. Her happiness is mine.

I weep as I write, for of all the cats with whom I once shared the house over the years, Tabsy possesses all the qualities one could wish for in a feline friend. Her timing is impeccable. She is there to comfort and lend her support at the exact moment and in a way where a man or woman, however well-meaning, could only add to my underlying disappointment in the human race of which I am a somewhat disaffected member.

I love her dearly, and identify totally with the comment Dudley Moore made to me at his London home, many years ago: "I was more upset when one of these cats died than when my bass player committed suicide". I don't believe for one moment Dudley was being callous towards his bass player over whom he shed that genuine tear while listening to an album in my Wanstead flat, way back in the early 70s. But his heart-felt remark perfectly illustrates the mystic marvel of a cat's hold over a sensitive human soul. No wonder the ancient Egyptians regarded the cat as a sacred animal.

But back to Tabsy. I will never forget the occasion when she 'played' my Steinway grand during a very busy night – on July 3rd, 1997, to be exact…

As my barboy Raul busied himself serving drinks, I entertained to a full house. I had just finished a jazz up-tempo number and was about to embark upon the next, in true segue form, when Tabsy, who had been watching me closely from the nearby staircase overlooking the piano, ran down the stairs, jumped on to my lap, anchored her hind legs firmly on my own legs, lifted her body against my chest and her paws over the keys, and smartly 'bashed' some notes with her right paw, and another set with her left in quick succession. She wanted to play the piano, and show off like her friend Tony, or perhaps she was simply upstaging me. She did just that. The place was in uproar. A joyous and astonished crowd round the piano looked on as Tabsy jumped down from my lap, and refused an encore. But she had done it, bless her. She had done it.

On other occasions, she would sit on the piano top as I played to an attentive audience. At the end of the set, she'd walk elegantly up to me while I received the applause. And as I stroked her with affection and kissed her on the head, she'd take her own individual 'bow'. Other nights she'd sit directly in front of me while I played a romantic ballad, and look lovingly in my eyes, and smile. Then she'd raise a paw and touch my face... Yes, she smiles, my little Tabs. So many of my customers are enamoured with the way she smiles. She does this if she likes you, and you like her. Cats know, don't they? But Tabsy, for me, is a one-off.

On the night before the fourth closure of my bar, when the police entered to deliver their puny piece of paper from The Town Hall and my customers sighed with exasperation and disbelief that *four* policemen were needed to close me in such an arbitrary fashion (while my neighbour sat smugly in her 'eerie' abroad, presumably out of ear-shot even of my piano playing) Tabsy walked straight up to me, as I got on serving the customers behind the bar, to give me her love and support. She didn't want food. But she wanted to express her feelings. What a cat.

Now, as I write and listen to a CD of Ashkenazy playing Rachmaninoff, I look round and see Tabsy listening, too. And whilst there is a vast difference between this great Russian pianist and Sharp, even I would admit, *I* feed Tabsy. Ashkenazy does not. So she chooses to live with me and put up with my music. Bless her little heart, she often ambles across my piano to sit near during my practice hour, and look me straight in the eye with love. She picks her favourites, of course, from a selection of jazz, ballads or Chopin preludes; and is still my best friend.

The very day Tabs died, May 25th 2004, two stunning-looking girls entered my bar and brought their individual love and support. If I had closed the business that night, only to mope around the place on my own, what would be the point? I had decided it was better to be surrounded by people, preferably by those of a sensitive nature. I was not to be disappointed.

The mother of one of the girls had a friend who ran The Spiritualist Association of Great Britain of which I am a member; and to think I'd never seen these girls before in my life. They were each so intuitive... Another lady sat at the bar, giving out rays of love and sympathy. 'God *knows* you are in pain, Tony,' she said with genuine and quiet understanding. 'Be strong. You will see Tabsy again.'

That night, as I lay in bed, feeling decidedly bereft and alone, the bed suddenly shook as this being jumped on the top and snuggled up to me. I could even feel the soft fur on my neck. No, you naughty reader, it wasn't one of those sexy girls. It was Tabsy, I am convinced.

Another night, about a week later, I could not go to sleep, grieving for my cat. With my face drenched in tears, I wept continuously and lay awake for a whole hour, alone in my big bed, pining for my Tabs. Suddenly, the bed shook beneath me, the weight of a cat fell strongly on my feet and a little white ghost appeared, encompassed by a delicate blue border. It was so beautiful. I watched with fascination and awe as it raised itself from my feet and drifted slowly and steadily towards the bar – next to which I would pull out my bed every night when the customers had left and I'd locked up. The apparition continued on its course, and as it gently disappeared into the bar tiles, I spoke softly in its direction: 'Thank you, Tabsy.' I stopped crying immediately and fell into a much needed, peaceful slumber.

The following year, I sold the bar, and moved up into the mountains. Who knows where I will go next before my earthly life ends? It matters not, for I have my beliefs that give me more than a morsel of comfort. As for ghosts, earth-bound or otherwise, I have seen so many (and had a witness to one) that an after-life, to my mind, is so normal and natural a concept that I wonder why people have ceased to wonder at *this* one.

In the meantime, my darling Tabsy, I have been told, is waiting for me to 'pop off' before she properly joins the spirit world. She'd rather remain with me. I feel the same about her and take pleasure and comfort in the thought of her travelling with me wherever I go. In fact, on December 27th 2004, after spending Christmas with my family in London, I was sitting in the front row of an Easy Jet aeroplane at Gatwick airport, waiting for the stewardess to close the front passenger door to enable us to start taxiing for take-off. We were all aboard with safety-belts tightened, eager for our getaway back to Spain, when a little tabby cat came running along the boarding corridor, tail up, and into the cabin... 'Wait for *me*,' she seemed to say. I watched as she disappeared into the ether of the aircraft, and the girl closed the door for departure.

Of course, I kept quiet about what I'd seen. It was, after all, a private matter between Tabs and me.

And still the magic continues, for in my house, here in the mountains, I feel the presence of Tabsy as the weight of her 'body' presses down on my feet when I lie in bed. She does this when I least expect it and when, I suspect, she judges it appropriate. For she knows that whilst I've grown very fond of my new house cat, I still love her – Tabsy, my soul-mate – and will never say goodbye.

CHAPTER 32

I had long dreamt of owning a wacking great Steinway Concert Grand, not specifically for the purpose of annoying my neighbour, but for the thrill of its powerful grandeur, subtle nuances, great action, and means of artistic expression.

Years ago, on a rare visit to John Lill – soon to win The Tchaikovsky Prize in Moscow and become a famous concert pianist – I was treated to a glimpse of a very special world of music. John sat at his Steinway grand in his mother's house in East London, and got down to some serious stuff. I could hardly believe the power of that piano, induced by John's marvellous, passionate playing. After stepping back a fair number of paces in the large room, in order to preserve my then precious hearing, I moved forward again to the piano at what I fancied to be an appropriate moment.

'This is Mozart, isn't it, John?' Perhaps a touch of unsolicited cynicism in my voice prompted his response...

'Yes. He was a *man*, not a bloody sissy.'

I quickly warmed to John. Liked his style. We Londoners tend not to mince words.

'What about the neighbours?' I continued.

'Bloody blacks,' he replied. 'They make enough bloody row, themselves.'

I loved it. There was no silly, stifling political correctness in those days, watched over by a sanctimonious Prime Minister on whatever side of an ever-diminishing, blurred fence. Not even misplaced malice. Just plain, straightforward speaking. A spade was a spade.

I never did find out whether family arguments, a steel band or bongos were the springboards of John Lill's remark. No doubt, if the late Oscar Peterson in his prime had been his neighbour then, an agreeable accommodation of interests and perhaps more could have been achieved, and a good time had by all. "Bloody blacks" would no longer apply.

In those days, of course, I was 'high' on the harpsichord, and went on to give those recitals in The Purcell Room, London, and show up for a number of appearances on BBC2, playing my own form of jazz, before mucking up my career and having a very interesting time doing it. Flirting with Hammond organs, Fender Rhodes electric pianos and an assorted array of other, more modern noises would, however, bring me eventually back to 'steam' piano. A Steinway Grand gives me all I want.

My black baby was a full-size concert grand, Model 'D', made in Hamburg in the peaceful times of 1901, years before the Americans ever thought of bombing their own factories in a day-light raid. God knows where the piano is, now, for I sold it when I 'retired'. It just would not fit into the little house I felt was meant for me. I bought an upright Schimmel, but still pine for another Steinway. Maybe I'll have to wait to play God's or even The Devil's.

Anyway, when the authorities allowed me to open my bar in Nirvana to alcoholics, as long as I did not play the piano in public, I carried on practising during the day and on my night off. So, come 2001, there would surely be a party to celebrate the hundredth birthday of the Steinway. I decided to give a recital to some close friends. What a night...

We opened quite a few bottles of good cava, and a delicious home-made cake with 100 neatly and thoughtfully iced upon it was provided by one of my guests. I cannot be sure whether this was a sly reference to me and my condition rather than that of the piano who seemed to care not a whit about her age. She sounded superb. I wonder if certain other makes of piano would sound as good, after a hundred years of travel and being bashed upon by all kinds of acrobats.

That morning I had tidied up the place and polished the body of the piano, but omitted to clean and polish the keys. When I sat down to play for my friends in the evening, I noticed *someone* had been at work. Now, no one could possibly have entered the house without my knowing. Besides, would he or she have bothered to polish the keys so thoroughly? I would not put it past my aunt Bet, always a determined lady, to have obtained a special dispensation from the other world to polish them for me, with love… Altogether, the event was a great success, and rounded off with a first-class dinner in my favourite restaurant. If the piano is as good in another hundred years (wherever it may be), I, like aunt Bet, would be only too happy to seek that dispensation to polish the keys for the birthday.

I must be thankful for small mercies, I suppose, for between one stressful closure and another there were several compensatory nights when I'd be lucky enough to hold a wonderful audience in the palm of my hand: always a gratifying experience for a musician, and worth savouring. Then other players would give the public a rest from old Sharp: their styles would range from delicate to 'shocking'. All good fun… Oh, is that another string broken? Damn.

One of my casual customers, a fine jazz pianist of some forty odd summers, made the appreciative remark one night, after enjoying himself playing a few standards on my piano: 'She's like an old Bentley, isn't she?'

I suppose that was about right. Except I'd add a touch of Ferrari or Maserati when I got going: that wonderful growl that comes and goes in the bass register. Only a Steinway does this. Maybe it's that 'OOMPH' that excited my neighbour into denouncing me over and over again...

I just know my problems with her could have been sorted years ago. But as I have already implied, Himmler in Drag hardly turns me on. And a bag over the head, in my humble opinion, should be reserved for Spanish fiestas or meetings of the Ku Klux Klan. Moreover, with all due respect, who would want a piano bar to resemble Hitler's bunker in order to cut a few measly decibels?

God knows how I survived it all. Talk about the blues: even my close family back in England, members of whom have observed my dramatic, chequered career since my birth a thousand years ago would never have imagined what was happening to me and my Steinway. Nirvana was purported to offer peace and civilized living to those who chose to reside here. But The Devil comes in pretty packages, and people are people.

And now all that, I hope, is a thing of the past. There is just old age to cope with. I try to remain cheerful, and keep things simple, for I see no point in cluttering one's life, worrying about matters which will never change or over which one has little or no control. Life is too short for such complications. Reading, writing my books, playing my piano – complicated enough, and a good social life is all I convince myself I need.

If we need rain, we go into the streets and pray for it. Way back in the mid 90s, there was a serious rain shortage, here in the south. The people of Malaga prayed hard. The following year, The Man in the Sky opened his substantial flies and let us have it. Six weeks, almost non-stop. With his washer repaired, we would have been content with the usual two to three weeks average a year. But December of 2009 together with January and February of 2010 presented us a massive 'blip' of almost continual rain to keep us guessing. For who knows what climate change will do to Spain? The world seems a bit topsy-turvy, to say the least, though *I* shall not be here to see Martin Amis's prediction of a New Ice Age come to fruition.

When one is young, it's normal and healthy to enjoy 'now' and look to the future. When one is old, it is not necessarily such a dreadful thing to look back and ponder the past over a glass or two, and forget the bloody gout. A human being is not a common motor car, a tool with which to get from A to B, to be serviced and given an oil change or consigned to the crusher before its time. One should be free to choose an individual path, for life is a mosaic of ebb and flow, yin and yang, rough and smooth, laughter and tears. Some of us can cope, some cannot. And *still* the sun shines on the just and wicked alike. Do you imagine there to be an exception to this rule? In Nirvana?

Printed in Great Britain
by Amazon